The All-New

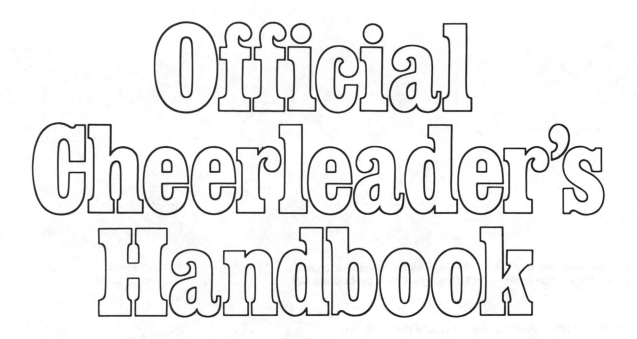

Official Cheerleader's Handbook

**Randy L. Neil and
Elaine Hart**

with the Staff of
The International Cheerleading
Foundation, Inc.

A FIRESIDE BOOK
Published by Simon & Schuster, Inc. ● New York

This is a revised edition of *The Official Cheerleader's Handbook,* originally
published by Fireside Books in 1979. Copyright © 1979 by Randolph Neil

Revised Fireside Edition, 1986

Published by Simon & Schuster, Inc.

Simon & Schuster Building
Rockefeller Center
1230 Avenue of the Americas
New York, New York 10020

FIRESIDE and colophon are registered trademarks of Simon & Schuster, Inc.

Manufactured in the United States of America

10 9 8 7 6

Library of Congress Cataloging in Publication Data
Neil, Randy
    The all-new official cheerleader's handbook.

    Rev. ed. of: The official cheerleader's handbook /
Randy L. Neil and the staff of the International
Cheerleading Foundation, Inc. c1979.
    "A Fireside book."
    1. Cheerleading-Handbooks, manuals, etc.   I. Hart,
Elaine.   II. Neil, Randy. Official cheerleader's
handbook.   III. International Cheerleading Foundation.
IV. Title
LB3635.N46   1986   791'.64   86-6621
ISBN: 0-671-61210-7

To the staff of the International Cheerleading Foundation—past and present—for their loyal support and their belief that cheerleaders really can make a difference.

Contents

Contents

Acknowledgments

Behind the preparation of this book are many fine people and institutions. This book is the result of the efforts of the several thousand young people who have given their ideas and work to the International Cheerleading Foundation since its inception in 1964. This is not just "our" cheerleading book. It is the book of the ICF and the tens of thousands of cheerleaders who have been trained by us over the years.

A special note of appreciation is extended to Allyn Miller and Judi Lamberth. Allyn spent many hours working on the original manuscript, but of greater importance were the many years she worked, helping ICF become one of the largest youth training programs in America. Her diligence and contributions greatly affected the success of the ICF. Judi has also devoted years of work to the ICF, and we are forever grateful. She is an outstanding educator whose competency in cheerleading curriculum and sponsor training programs has had a tremendous impact on the proficiency of cheerleading as we know it today.

Of constant assistance in the writing of our original manuscript was Katie Stolz. We are forever appreciative of her commitment to excellence and the never-ending dedication she gave to the completion of the handbook.

Several others—all experts in training cheerleaders—have devoted their time and energy to the revised edition, including Scott Cusimano, Karla Tenbrink, Dan Cleveland, Debbie Knapp, and Chris Kirby. Scott is the ICF's Head Consultant in Cheering Skills. His expertise in the field is unsurpassed. Chris assists Scott and excels in developing and teaching cheerleading athletic skills. We appreciate Debbie's research and consultation in the aerobic training and conditioning requirements for cheerleaders. And Dan and Karla, both full-time professionals in the field, are proficient and highly skilled in developing and training high school and collegiate cheerleaders.

We thank the models from Scott's gym, Kipper's Gymnastic Club, Ardmore, Oklahoma, those from the Elite Gymnastic Club of Overland Park, Kansas, the varsity cheerleaders Chris coaches at the University of Arizona, and the varsity cheerleaders from Orange Park High School *(Florida)* (cover photograph). We also thank the members of our staff and the many cheerleading squads whose pictures appear in the handbook.

We offer devoted thanks to the many photographers who assisted with this project. Chief among these individuals in Bill Lindsay, our talented and competent staff photographer. Bob Fussell, Tom Rowe, Mark Noe, Malcolm Smith, and Robert F. Walker all contributed their photography skills. We especially appreciate the work of our cover photographer, Steve Williams, of Visual Sports Network, Jacksonville, Florida, and artist Mark Schuler, for the beautiful painting on the back cover. The following schools have offered special assistance: University of Minnesota; Florida State University; University of Kansas; University of North Carolina; University of Arizona; Kansas State University; Rockhurst College; William Chrisman High School, Independence, Missouri; Park Hill High School, Parkville, Missouri; Orange Park High School, Orange Park, Florida; Etowah High School, Attalla, Alabama; Bainbridge High School, Bainbridge, Georgia; and Saks High School, Anniston, Alabama.

To everyone contributing to this project and to the International Cheerleading Foundation's continued efforts to improve cheerleading in America, we thank you.

Randy Neil and Elaine Hart
Fall 1985

Introduction

The Official Cheerleader's Handbook is the grand total of twenty-two years of gathering ideas, techniques, and methods dealing with the entire spectrum of school spirit in America. We believe that cheerleaders are natural leaders who have emerged from the sea of students in a school. If motivated and trained properly, a cheerleader's leadership and physical potential is limitless—today within the school, tomorrow within families, friends, the work place, communities, and governments.

Are you interested in becoming a cheerleader? Or, would you like to become a better cheerleader? If so, this book was written especially for you. We have carefully outlined what it takes, both mentally and physically, to prepare for cheerleading. The physical side of cheerleading is extremely strenous. As in all sports, cheerleading requires tremendous dedication, preparation, knowledge of the sport, and a close regard for safety and injury prevention.

Follow the instructions given in this book to learn the basic cheerleading skills (jumps, gymnastics, stunts, etc.). If you would like to further improve you physical ability, try working with a qualified gymnastics coach, dance instructor, or an experienced cheerleader. And, for a week-long training camp in cheerleading, contact the ICF (International Cheerleading Foundation, Shawnee Mission, Kansas). We offer excellent, professional instruction across the nation for anyone who is serious about improving their cheerleading skills.

Cheerleaders are seriously affecting the attitudes within schools and communities across America. As more cheerleaders understand the importance of their leadership, school spirit and pride will continue to grow. The ICF motto, "Attitude Leads to Excellence," is shared by cheerleaders everywhere. Lead with a positive attitude; choose to be enthusiastic; choose to be determined and organized; and make something happen at your school! We are proud to be a part of cheerleading in America and we encourage you to work to become the best cheerleader you can be! GOOD LUCK!

1
The History of Cheerleading

The history of cheering goes as far back as the late 1880's when the first organized, recorded yell was performed on an American campus: "RAY, RAY, RAY! TIGER, TIGER, TIGER! SIS, SIS, SIS! BOOM, BOOM, BOOM! Aaaaaah! PRINCETON, PRINCETON, PRINCETON!," done in locomotive style, was first seen and heard during a college football game.

In 1884, Thomas Peebles, a graduate of Princeton University, took that yell, *and* the sport of football (actually derived from rugby), to the University of Minnesota. It was from that campus that organized cheerleading came into being.

Cheerleading, as we know it today, was initiated in 1898 by Johnny Campbell, an undergraduate at the University of Minnesota, who stood before the crowd at a football game and directed them in a famous, and still-used yell, "RAH, RAH, RAH! SKU-U-MAH, HOO-RAH! HOO-RAH! VARSITY! VARSITY! MINN-E-SO-TAH!"

Johnny Campbell's innovation of cheerleading was documented by the following story that appeared in the November 12, 1898, edition of a Minnesota student publication, *Ariel:* "The following were nominated to lead the yelling today: Jack [sic] Campbell, F. G. Kotlaba, M. J. Luby, Albert Armstrong of the Academics; Wickersham of the Laws; and Litzenberg of the Medics. These men should see to it that everybody leaves the park today breathless and voiceless— as this is the last game here, it ought to be a revelation to the people of Minneapolis in regard to University enthusiasm."

And so cheerleading officially began on November 2, 1898.

In the fall of 1919, some of America's greatest universities were just then becoming "great." For some reason, in those days, greatness was whether or not your university had a big, big football stadium. A stadium could accommodate large crowds, and large crowds helped to build good football teams—and the better your football team, the more attention you could attract to your school. Attention was the name of the game, and if you could attract it, then your university could build itself into an important *educational* institution as well as being good in sports.

It was a "do or die" situation for the University of Kansas. For years their football team (the "Jayhawks") had been playing in rickety old McCook Stadium, which had seats for only 2,000 people. Very few of the "big football teams" would come to play at Kansas because the crowds were so small.

On a cold autumn afternoon, a great story of cheerleadership was about to unfold. And it took a great cheerleader to engineer what was about to be a massive job. His name was Shirley Windsor (that's right, Shirley was a guy, for in those days, very few women were cheerleaders) and his squad numbered only three individuals.

Kansas had been invited to Lincoln, Nebraska, to play the nationally ranked University of Nebrasks Cornhuskers. An awesome task for any football team, and especially so for the Jayhawks because the Cornhuskers outweighed the KU team by nearly twenty pounds per man.

Head coach Forrest Allen took his team to Nebraska and on a wet, cold playing field, they fought hard. In fact, they fought so well that the game's final score ended in a surprising tie, 20-20. And KU might even have won the game if a touchdown in the final minute of play had not been called back by the referee.

The Jayhawks came back to Kansas riding on a tide of enthusiasm that had never before happened to them. They were greeted by thousands of cheering students as their train pulled into the depot.

Realizing what the situation could mean, Shirley Windsor called various influential former KU students on the phone. He was asking for money to build a big stadium. After calls to Wichita, Topeka, Kansas City . . . Shirley had been turned down cold.

There was only one thing left to do.

Rushing up the steps of the KU administration building two at a time, Shirley asked to see the Chancellor of the university. He said, "Sir, if you would give your permission to stop all classes for one hour tomorrow morning, I think we could have the greatest pep rally this school has ever seen."

The Chancellor gave his okay to the idea, and the next morning Shirley and his two fellow cheerleaders watched as the 4,000 students of the university filed into Robinson Gymnasium.

"Our team has given us a great victory," explained Shirley. "Now is the time to build KU's first giant stadium so we can begin a football tradition at Kansas. But our alumni in cities around Kansas have turned us down. Will you help?"

After thirty minutes of rousing cheers and ceaseless noise, the 4,000 students of the University of Kansas pledged sixty dollars per person of *their own money* (that was truly a lot in those days), and nearly a quarter of a million dollars was raised in one short hour!

Two years later, on another cold, wet autumn afternoon, KU played Nebraska again. This time in the brand-new Memorial Stadium—30,000 seats! And one of America's great college sports traditions was born.

Other great traditions in the art of cheerleading have developed over the years. The following list highlights the major events in cheerleading history:

1870s The first pep club was established at Princeton University.

1880s The first organized yell was recorded at Princeton University.

1890s Organized cheerleading was initiated at the University of Minnesota, as was the first school "fight song."

1900s Usage of the megaphone was becoming popular, (When the megaphone was invented is not known, but it *was* in use on the day cheerleading began in 1898.) The first cheerleader fraternity, Gamma Sigma, was organized.

1910 The first "homecoming" was held at the University of Illinois.

1920s Women became active in cheerleading. the University of Minnesota cheerleaders began to incorporate gymnastics and tumbling into their cheers. The first flash-card cheering section was directed by Lindley Bothwell at Oregon State University. *Just Yells,* the first book on cheerleading, was written by Willis Bugbee and published.

1930s Universities and high schools began performing pom-pon routines and using paper pompons.

1940s The first cheerleading company was formed by Lawrence R. Herkimer of Dallas, Texas. The first national organization for cheerleaders was formed by Bill Horan—the American Cheerleaders Association.

1950s College cheerleaders began conducting cheerleading workshops to teach fundamental cheerleading skills.

1960s The vinyl pompon was invented by Fred Gasthoff and introduced by the International Cheerleading Foundation. The "Bruin High Step" style of pompon routine was developed by the UCLA cheerleaders and the International Cheerleading Foundation.

1967 marked the first annual ranking of the "Top Ten College Cheer Squads" and the initiation of the "Cheerleader All America" awards by the International Cheerleading Foundation.

In addition to cheering for the traditional football and basketball teams, cheerleaders began supporting all school sports, sometimes selecting several different squads to cheer for such as wrestling, track, and swimming.

1970s The first nationwide television broadcast of the National Collegiate Cheerleading Championships on CBS-TV in the spring of 1978, initiated by the International Cheerleading Foundation.

Cheerleading began to receive recognition as a serious athletic activity as the skill level dramatically increased in areas such as gymnastics, partner stunts, pyramids, and advanced jumps.

Many high school cheerleading squads began cheering for female sports (basketball, volleyball) in addition to male sports.

Training for cheerleading coaches was offered at summer cheerleading camps.

Several colleges considered cheerleading a sport and offered scholarships, college credits, and a four-year letter program.

1980s National cheerleading competitions for junior and senior high school as well as collegiate squads took place across the nation.

The International Cheerleading Foundation's Training Course for faculty cheerleading sponsors and coaches was offered across the nation during the school year.

Cheerleaders increased their involvement with community service projects.

Cheerleaders received national media recognition as one of the most important school leadership groups to promote enthusiastic, positive attitudes and school spirit within schools and communities.

Cheerleading has come a long way in ten decades. The importance of cheerleading has also come a long way and was first acknowledged by Willis Bugbee in 1927, when he wrote:

"The cheerleader, where once merely tolerated, is now a person of regal estate. His prestige is such that in many schools and colleges he must win his place through competitive examinations."

And it is true today, that a person must be highly skilled and competitive in order to achieve the honored and respected position of cheerleader. This cherished position has, throughout the years, been held by some truly famous, talented people. The list includes former President Dwight D. Eisenhower, actor Jimmy Stewart, actress Cheryl Ladd, and former Miss America Phyllis George, to name a few.

Whether you are a cheerleader, a yell leader, a songleader or a spirit leader (variations of the term "cheerleader"), whether you are on an all-female squad, an all-male squad or a combination male/female squad, you are striving toward one goal. That goal is to effectively lead a crowd in their support of an athletic team and to generate spirit and pride within a school and community.

Today cheerleading enjoys the reputation of being an important leadership force on practically every high school and college campus in the nation. All of this is because of a man in Minnesota who couldn't stand sitting in the bleachers. He had to be in front of them! Thank you, Johnny Campbell!

2

Qualifications

The activity of cheerleading has dramatically changed over the years, especially in the '70s and '80s. It is NOT the "social activity" of old. Cheerleaders are important school leaders and athletes.

Since cheerleading is one of the most important and respected school activities, it is essential that the right people be selected for the job. Special qualifications, which are described in detail later in the chapter, must be met. To help determine whether you meet the preliminary qualifications necessary to become a cheerleader, we have prepared a short quiz for you. Be sure to answer all the questions honestly:

PHYSICAL CONDITION	YES	NO
1. Are you in good health?	____	____
2. Is your weight satisfactory?	____	____
3. Are you satisfied with your general appearance?	____	____
4. Are you coordinated in physical activities?	____	____

SCHOOL ACTIVITIES		
1. Do you have a "C" average or better?	____	____
2. Are you willing to devote time and energy to extra-curricular acitvities?	____	____
3. Do you stick with school projects and assignments from start to finish, no matter what happens?	____	____
4. Do you believe that your education is of the greatest importance?	____	____

YOUR PERSONALITY		
1. Do you get along with, and work well with, other people?	____	____
2. Are you able to control your emotions?	____	____
3. Do you have an outgoing, energetic personality?	____	____
4. Do you have a confident, positive opinion of yourself?	____	____
5. Can you fairly give and maturely accept criticism?	____	____
6. Are you an enthusiastic fan who honestly enjoys sports?	____	____
7. Are you dependable?	____	____
8. Do you feel you are a good representative of your school?	____	____

If you answered "no" to any of these questions, you need to work on improving that area. All of these qualities and their importance are described below:

Physical Condition. Cheerleading is a strenuous athletic activity, much like soccer or basketball. A well-organized conditioning program is a must for anyone who plans to be an effective cheerleader. This means that every muscle in your body must be ready to do the job. Weak backs or "bad knees" have no place on a cheerleading squad. In fact, you would probably only make the condition worse and it might have harmful effects on you later in life. If you have an ailment such as asthma or migraine headaches you should seriously consider how cheerleading could affect you and your squad. If you are prone to illness or injury, you will more than likely become the one weak link, or member, of your squad.

Along with your overall physical condition, your weight is important. Anyone who is seriously over- or underweight will not be in shape to participate in exciting physical events. You should certainly correct that figure fault before thinking of cheerleading. Corrections should involve the establishment of proper health and nutrition habits.

Coordination is another key item which falls under the category of physical condition. Very often one has to work hard to develop coordination (the ability to achieve rhythm . . . matching what you do with someone else's movements). If you are one of those people not blessed with natural coordination, there is definitely something you can do to correct it: 1) get yourself a metronome and practice motions to the beat of the metronome's back-and-forth arm; 2) have a friend or professional instructor teach you to dance; 3) Practice your cheers, jumps, etc., in front of a mirror with another cheerleader who performs as you would like to. Practice over and over until awkward movements become more familiar and natural.

School Activities. Your grades are of the utmost importance. You will find that large amounts of time will be spent away from studies so that you can work on various projects and games. If your grades aren't good now, they will suffer even more when you become a cheerleader. You should learn to budget your time and keep up with your assignments from the very day they are given. Being a good student will also help you to become a more organized, alert cheerleader.

As you probably already know, schoolwork doesn't mean just classes and studies. There are clubs, student government, committees and all sorts of other activities that make your school into a true "community."

As School Leaders . . . Cheerleaders are responsible for the spirit programs within a school and community. Ideally, an excellent spirit program makes a positive difference in the entire atmosphere surrounding a school. Cheerleaders provide the "glue" that brings together various school groups, faculty members, and the community. Most school activity groups focus on one area only but cheerleaders focus on EVERYONE ELSE as well as themselves! They are concerned with the attitude, unity, and spirit of their school as they support the achievements of all others.

As School Athletes . . . Cheerleaders now find their activity considered a true athletic event complete with physical conditioning requirements, performances, competitions, safety hazards, and tests of human endurance and strength common to all sports. The more skilled a squad becomes as a performing unit, the more a crowd will respect and support the cheerleaders' spirit-raising efforts.

Do You Have What It Takes? That is the first question to ask yourself as you consider becoming a cheerleader! Congratulations! It is not an easy undertaking but the rewards are many.

Cheerleading is Hard Work. Plenty of sacrifice is required to increase spirit at your school. You will have to give much more than you take and there is no room for lazy or selfish people.

Cheerleading is Self-Discipline. You will dedicate your entire year to live up to the standards, goals, and rules of your squad. Your school work must come first, but cheerleading is next. You will have little time for anything else!

Cheerleading is Teamwork. Do you work well with others? You will spend many hours with your teammates—lots of hard work, aching muscles, tears, frustrations, criticisms, and plenty of fun, smiles, and laughter. You must care enough about your squad to be able to listen, to learn from criticism, improve your mistakes, and be patient through the long hours of practice until everyone gets it right.

Cheerleading is Public Relations. You not only need to work well with your teammates, cheerleaders also must cooperate with sponsors, administrators, students, and the community. You will become a liaison between the team, the officials, and the crowd. It is up to you to organize and direct the spirit of the crowd; but first, you'll need to create that spirit! You need to determine whether you are an "I'll Help Out" person or a "Forget It, Let Someone Else Do It" person. If you are the latter, you would not enjoy being a cheerleader.

Dedication is another important quality that all cheerleaders should possess. Dedication means sticking to something no matter what happens or how bad things may seem. If your team is having an off year, it is up to you to generate school spirit and let your team members know that their school is behind them all the way. You can't be a quitter, nor can you fake your dedication and sincerity. One of the greatest personal rewards you will experience as a cheerleader is the appreciation of your team for your sincere support, whether they are winning or losing.

Your Personality. A cheerleader must be an energetic, outgoing person with an ability to lead and charm an audience. You cannot be timid, but you should never be overbearing. Making friends should come easily to you and you should always have a pleasant smile for everyone (even if you're in a bad mood). You must be able to control your emotions and be a good winner, as well as a good loser.

Since the main goal of a cheerleader is perfection, it is important for you to be able to give and take constructive criticism along the way. You should make it a personal rule to criticize others the way you, yourself, would like to be criticized.

Self-discipline and dependability are two other important qualities of the oustanding cheerleader. You must discipline yourself to make sacrifices, which may mean giving up going to a show so you can attend a poster making party, etc. You must also be dependable by being on time, keeping yourself in shape, following through on all cheerleading assignments given you, looking your best and being the best school representative you can.

In the days you will spend preparing to become a cheerleader, here are some tips to keep in mind that will aid you in your role as a cheerleader:

1. A cheerleader is a student *first,* before anything else. Make sure you do well in school. Strive to make good grades. Be attentive to your teachers and helpful to them when you can.

2. Watch for school activities that are particularly suited to your own special talents. If you are good at art, then volunteer to make posters for homecoming, or decorating the floats for the parade. If you are a good public speaker, join the debate team. And if your school gets involved in a charity drive, make sure you can help out.

3. Develop good clothing and grooming habits. Read up on things; take a look at the people around you. When you look well, you set an example for everyone you know.

4. Know a little about your school's history and traditions. Every school has things in its past for which everyone should be proud. Before you can be truly proud of your school, you should know some of the great incidents in its past. For instance, does your school have a high academic record? What were your school's best football and basketball seasons? When was your school founded? Find out about the person for whom your school is named. Look through some of the old school yearbooks.

5. Choose your friends well. Many young people want to do things that are not right, like using drugs and alcoholic beverages. Encourage your friends not to do these things, and on all occasions, avoid them yourself.

6. Try to organize yourself. For example, make sure you are not late to classes. When you're assigned to do something, do it well and *on time.* Develop a reputation for being a "doer," not a "goof-off."

7. Smile. Is there anything more contagious?

8. Command the respect of the adults around you. Your teachers, your parents, the adults you know in your community. Be helpful and attentive when you are around them.

9. And most important of all: make yourself the ranking expert on cheerleading in your school. Know all the rules by heart. Know every cheer so that you can almost do them in your sleep. Become familiar with every activity in which the cheerleaders in your school are involved.

3

Conditioning

Exercise and proper nutrition are the keys to a well-conditioned body. Since cheerleading is such a strenuous activity, it cannot be well executed by a person who is out of shape or undernourished.

You need to begin working as early as possible to develop the smoothness, strength, endurance, poise, and grace of movement that is essential to cheerleading. Included later in this chapter are some basic exercises that will get you started. Don't be disappointed if your form does not immediately match that of the model in the pictures. Only dedication and regular practice can develop flexibility and control.

YOUR FITNESS PROGRAM

Although you cannot alter your body structure, you can improve your coordination and muscle tone. You can begin by setting up an exercise schedule and work out for at least 30 minutes. A fitness program should be done a minimum of three days a week in order to develop and maintain a level of fitness. To increase your fitness level, increase the number of days a week you work out, the length of time you work out and/or the intensity of your workout, i.e., adding hand weights while doing aerobics or working on arms or increasing the tension on your exercise bicycle. You can add running, jumping rope, aerobic dance, bicycling, or light calisthenics once you feel comfortable with the basic warm-up and conditioning exercises (FIT = Frequency, Intensity, and Time.) Everyone should have a complete physical checkup by his or her personal physician to make sure that there are no restrictions on what exercises you can do.

As you begin your exercise program, you can expect to have sore muscles. Don't overdo it the first day. Athletes are not made in one day. Use your judgment and work hard to make progress, but keep in mind that it takes time, patience, and practice to get your muscles in shape. As you do begin to acquire muscle tone, look for signs such as firming leg or stomach muscles.

Your fitness program should include a minimum of the following areas of training: flexibility, strength, and endurance. A warm-up period of 5 to 10 minutes is a must before going into any physical activity. You should warm up beginning at the top (head) and work your way down the body as illustrated later in this chapter. The only exception would be to warm up the feet and ankles, first, then go back to the legs, since several warm-up and stretches for the legs are done on the floor. The warm-up period is to raise the body temperature and prepare it for further activity. You should not work on flexibility, endurance, or strength training during these first few minutes.

ENDURANCE

Some type of aerobic exercise is a MUST for endurance. The point of aerobics is to do exercises that demand a lot of oxygen. The aim is to get the heart working hard so that by strenuous use it will get stronger and stronger. The heart rate must be raised and *maintained* to increase endurance. "Stop and go" exercises, i.e., basketball, racquetball, and tennis, are not aerobic. Begin with only a few minutes, five or less if need be, and work up to 20 or 25 minutes of aerobic time. WORK GRADU-ALLY! You did not get out of shape in a day; likewise, you should not expect to get into shape in a day or two. You should be able to talk to your neighbor without difficulty as you work out. If you cannot, your body is having to work too hard. Slow down. Take the uphill climb slowly and enjoy it! Some type of aerobic activity is essential in being able to freeze through a series of jumps, tumbling runs, or a tough dance routine at maximum performance and energy level with seemingly little effort.

FLEXIBILITY

Flexibility training should come at the end of your workout after the muscles are already warmed up. Stretching during the warm-up period at the beginning of your workout is done to increase your range of motion just enough to prepare for further activity. It helps prevent injuries such as muscle strains as it prevents tearing and pulling of muscle fibers and lessens irritations to muscle tendons. Stretching also helps coordination and balance because overall body movement and more rapid change of direction are easier.

Of all areas of fitness, flexibility is lost the most rapidly. It will come only if you stretch regularly. Concentrate on holding the stretch longer rather than doing lots of repetitions. Hold a stretch for a minimum of 20 seconds and as long as 30 to 60 seconds if possible. This static stretching helps the muscles get used to the stretched state. *Never* bounce when stretching. Muscles can be thought of as elastic or rubber bands. A quick jerk will result in pulling or tearing of the muscle fibers. Hold to the point of tightness and *never* to the point of pain. Bouncing will tighten you up, rather than make you more flexible. Stretch in a comfortable position. If it hurts, *don't do it!* If it's difficult, try!!

A good flexibility program involves *all* the major muscle groups of the body. Flexibility is joint specific, meaning you may be flexible in the leg and hip area, but tight in the shoulder region. Therefore, flexibility must be worked on at each specific area. There is no such thing as general flexibility. Never compare yourself to others. Each person is different and should be dealt with accordingly, as should the specific muscle group you are working on.

As you work on your flexibility, always breath and *relax* as much as possible. Never hold your breath or force the stretch. You may over-stretch and cause injury. Flexibility can be gained rapidly with consistency in effort and lost just as quickly if neglected. Don't take a chance. Take the time to stretch before and after activity, and you will decrease your chances of injury and the amount of soreness you will have later on, as well as enhance your levels of performance and fitness.

STRENGTH

Strength is defined as the quality of being strong, the ability to do or endure, and the power to resist attack. Strength is important to a cheerleader for a number of reasons. He/she needs the arm and leg strength to execute and hold a partner stunt or pyramid, the power to proficiently execute tumbling skills, as well as the strength and endurance to make it through an entire game or performance with lots of energy. Exercise and/or conditioning programs added to your daily routine will make you stronger, but what happens once your body adjusts and becomes stronger?

If you desire only to maintain that particular level of fitness, continue a three-day-a-week program for the same length of time per workout and the same degree of intensity. In order to strengthen a particular part of the body, *Frequency*, *Intensity*, and/or *Time* must be added to that particular body part. For example, to further strengthen and tone the arms, add push-ups or some weight training specifically for the arms. To strengthen the heart muscle, add some type of aerobic activity such as swimming laps, aerobic dance, or jumping rope, or increase the length or frequency of your workouts. In order to strengthen and tone the leg muscles, add certain exercises for the specific leg muscles you want to work. To progress even more, include weight training for the legs or add ankle weights to your leg exercises. Weight training can be very beneficial, but do not be concerned with the amount of weight that you work with. Be more concerned with the manner in which you do the repetitions—*slow and controlled;* use muscle, *not* momentum! Make sure the weight is enough to get resistance, but not so much that 12 to 15 repetitions are impossible. *Never* wear ankle weights when jogging, jumping rope, or doing aerobic dance. This puts added stress on the knees, feet, and ankles.

Proper alignment and foot placement is of utmost importance with repetitive pounding of the feet onto any surface. When you run, the force on the balls of the feet is *three times the body weight!* The feet should be underneath the body and the knees in front of you when jogging in place. Place the ball of the foot down and press through to the heel to keep the calf muscles stretched and to help absorb the impact shock and body weight.

INJURY PREVENTION

The shins do *not* have the ability to absorb impact shock. This is why we get shin splints. Shin splints are stress factures caused by either improper foot placement (i.e., constantly landing on the balls of the feet) and/or too much activity. Ice, aspirin, and wrapping will only lessen the pain. The only thing that will help heal is *time.* You *must* give that part of the body a rest in order for it to heal properly, particularly if the cause is overactivity. The most important thing you can do for your body is to learn proper technique, placement, and alignment.

You should be concerned more with injury prevention than learning the proper cure for the ailment. This method will keep you healthier, more active, more knowledgeable, and more of a benefit to your squad and your school. Any mechanical system will eventually fail if it is subject to overstress. The human body is no exception! Above all, listen to your body and don't overdo. Some days you will be stronger and more flexible than others. Days when you feel weaker and tighter, *don't push yourself!* The reason for these tougher days could result from added stress, lack of concentration, lack of sleep, poor eating habits, or a combination of these.

EATING HABITS

Your eating habits are as important to your physical, mental, and emotional condition as are exercises. Everything you eat directly affects how you look and feel. Eating habits are acquired early in life and are just that—habits! Stop for a minute and think of what you have eaten today. Is your appearance suffering because you do not eat correctly? The majority of weight problems result directly from: 1) lack of exercise; 2) overeating (snacking); 3) undereating (skipping meals); or 4) eating foods with little or no nutritional value. It is rare to find someone whose weight problem is due to a physiological disorder. If your diet includes large amounts of greasy food (french fries, onion rings, etc.), sugar (soft drinks, cookies, candy, etc.), or starchy foods (doughnuts, breaded foods), beware! This is not a healthy diet. The majority of these foods are not used by your body, but stored as excess fuel (fat). Vitamins, minerals, proteins, and carbohydrates are essential for proper bodily function and maintenance. Lack of one or more of these result in the body having to use other sources such as lean muscle tissue that the body needs.

You need to learn to control and think about what you are putting into your mouth. A cold, crisp apple is much more nutritious than a candy bar. A fresh chilled salad will benefit you much more than a hamburger, french fries, and a soft drink. Convenience is *not* always best. Learn to eat slowly and take reasonably sized portions. Try to avoid snacking between meals. If you have to snack, eat fresh fruit or vegetables. Sometimes a glass of water, tea, or a type of fruit juice will suffice. Whatever you do, do not "crash diet." Eat sensibly and build up your health while you are adjusting your weight.

Be more concerned and aware of the ratio between lean muscle mass and body fat *quality of weight),* rather than the numbers on the scales (quantity of weight). Muscle weighs more than fat. The more lean your body is, the more efficiently it burns fat. Your body make-up and muscle metabolism are directly related to diet and exercise.

If you go on a crash diet, your percentage of body fat will decrease, but your muscle tissue and muscle metabolism efficiency will decrease also. A "target diet" (eating a sensibly balanced diet with a somewhat limited calorie and limited fat intake) will decrease the percentage of body fat, maintain the same number of pounds of muscle tissue, and maintain the same muscle metabolism. Weight lifting maintains the percentage of body fat (unless you begin a more strict diet), increases the number of pounds of muscle tissue, and increases muscle metabolism efficiency. Adding physical activity of an aerobic nature will decrease the percentage of body fat, increase the number of pounds of muscle tissue, and increase muscle metabolism efficiency. The key is that oxygen must be present to burn fat. Aerobics means with oxygen. Again, the purpose of all aerobics is to do exercise that demands a lot of oxygen. If you decide you want to alter your muscle tone, take off inches, or increase your energy level, review these principles and remember that the saying "you are what you eat" does have substantial meaning. A healthy diet combined with exercise will help you to become a better individual with better attitudes, discipline, and outlook.

When done regularly, exercise gives us:

- More energy
- Greater ability to handle stress
- Less depression
- Fewer physical complaints
- More efficient digestion
- A better self-image and more self-confidence
- A more attractive, streamlined body, including more effective personal weight control
- Bones of greater strength
- More restful sleep
- Better concentration at work and at school

Head and Neck

Head and neck exercises should be done slowly, holding (static stretch) at each position. Move from position to position very slowly. Concentrate on relaxation as you stretch. These exercises are also beneficial to release tension in the head, neck, and shoulder area.

- Greater perseverance in all daily tasks
- Fewer aches and pains
- Weight loss
- A diminished waist
- Slimmer hips
- Thinner thighs
- Improved flexibility
- Increased muscle tissue and decreased body fat
- Improved mental ability and awareness
- Sustained health!

Now that you're motivated, let's begin! Included in this chapter are several basic exercises to get you started on your program. Work on all of them regularly and remember to stretch, not force. (Specific exercises for the various cheerleading activities are illustrated later in the book.) LET'S GO!!!!

Shoulders

Stand with your feet approximately shoulder width
apart, being sure to keep
your knees slightly bent.
Keep your body aligned:
shoulders over your hips
(don't lean forward), buttocks tight, and abdominals
tucked. Raise your shoul-
ders up and down, together
or alternately. Then, roll your
shoulders forward in large
circles, either alternately or
together. Repeat rolling
backward.

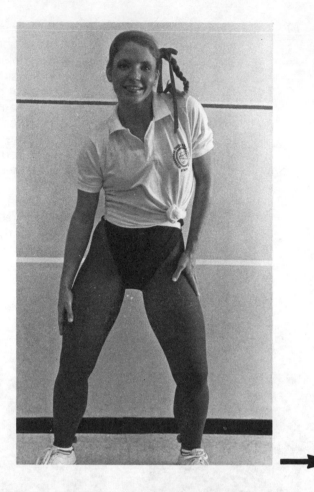

Arms and Wrists

TRICEPS
Put both arms behind your
head and grab the opposite
arm **above** the elbow. Gently
pull the arm to the opposite
side and hold. Repeat with
your other arm.

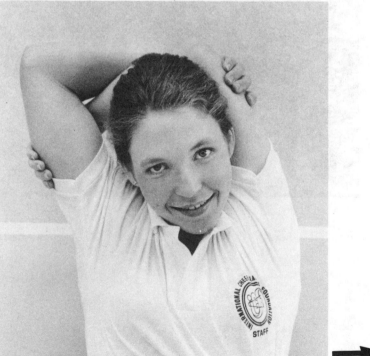

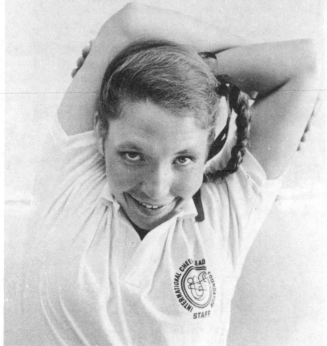

Wrists and Forearms

Kneel and place your hands in front of you with fingers facing your knees. Try to keep the heels of your hands on the floor. Hold this position several seconds. *Slowly,* shift the weight backwards, chest toward your thighs, hips toward your feet, keeping the heels of your hands toward the floor. Sit back far enough to gently stretch the wrists and forearms. Hold.

Sides

Stand with your feet approximately shoulder width apart, knees soft (bent slightly). Reach straight up, pressing the heel of your hand upward as much as possible so that you feel the stretch all the way down your side and into the lower abdominal area. Reach slowly and concentrate specifically on the stretch. Begin with four stretches on one side, then switch. Do two to each side for a few sets, then go to single reaches on each side if you choose.

Leg stretches

Inner thigh stretch: Sit with the feet together, arms crossed above the wrists, holding at the *ankles,* rather than the toes, and press knees toward the floor. Keep the body aligned, shoulders over the hips and abdominals tucked in, but keep the body relaxed.

Sit with one lower leg over the other and press the knees toward the floor. Lean forward far enough to feel the stretch in both the inner thigh of the lower leg and the top of the outer thigh of the top leg. Reach forward SLOWLY! Reach *forward* from the lower back rather than down with the shoulders. Repeat to the other side, switching legs.

Hamstring Stretch

Lie on your back, place one foot flat on the floor, and bring the other thigh to the chest and place your hands underneath the knee rather than on the knee to take the pressure off the joint. Slowly, extend the same leg and hold. Release slowly by simply bending the knee. Repeat to the same side two or three times, then repeat to the opposite leg. This exercise may also be done on the side as illustrated below. When lying on the side, the bottom leg should be brought forward slightly and the knee bent for better balance.

Modified Hurdle Stretch

Sit with one leg extended and the opposite foot tucked in to the extended inner thigh. Reaching forward, hold the stretch several seconds.

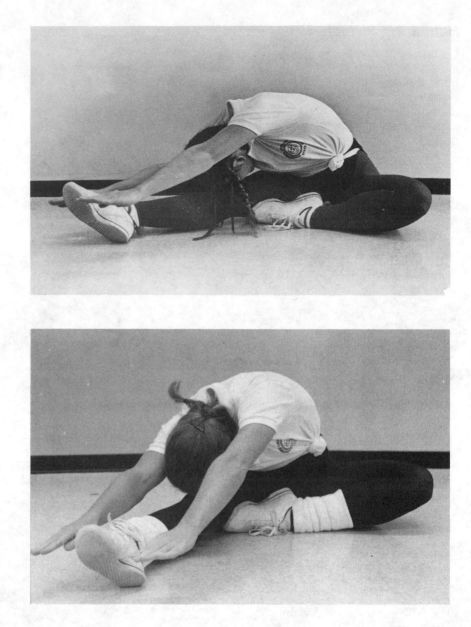

Continue to reach forward and stretch the calf also by flexing the foot and raising the head slightly and bringing the chin up toward the knee. Hold.

Slowly walk the hands forward and hold, keeping both hips on the floor. Slowly walk the hands toward the bent leg, place the lower arm behind the thigh for support, and reach *out* toward the opposite wall, stretching the side and releasing the hamstring muscles. Slowly return to an upright position. Repeat to the opposite side.

Straddle Stretch

Sit and straddle the legs to a *comfortable* position. Look and reach toward the foot. Hold several seconds.

b. Flex the foot slowly, raise the head slightly and bring the chin toward the knee. Hold several seconds and breathe!

c. Slowly walk the hands toward the center and continue reaching forward. Hold and relax.

d. Bring the hands forward slightly (continuing to reach forward further). Hold. Relax. Repeat inching forward slightly. Breathing is very important to effective stretching. Don't hold your breath. Do stretch GRADUALLY.

Hamstring

Sit in an upright position with the shoulders over the hips and the abdominals tucked in. Bring one thigh to the chest, hands *underneath,* with the opposite leg extended. Hold the bent leg to take stress off of the knee joint.

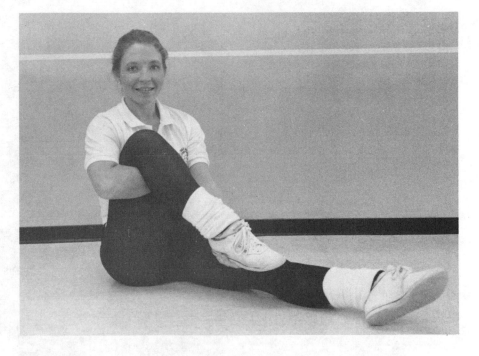

b. Slowly extend the bent leg, maintaining good posture. Hold several seconds.

c. Slowly lower the leg and the body at the same time, bringing the extended leg to the floor.

d. Hold, keeping both legs extended. Relax and breathe.

e. Slowly flex the feet and raise the head slightly, bringing the chin toward the knees. Hold.

f. Slowly lower the chest toward the thighs, reaching forward from the lower back. Hold. Release slowly, bending the knees and keeping the chin down and the back rounded as you roll up.

Runner's Stretch

a. Place the front foot *flat,* the knee directly above the ankle, giving support to the knee (a 90° angle). Extend the opposite leg behind, placing the hands on the floor for added support. DO NOT BOUNCE! Hold several seconds.

b. Slowly drop the back knee to the floor to stretch the quadricep (front of the thigh) a little further. Hold.

c. Keep the front foot in place, raise the hips, and slide the back foot forward, keeping both toes in the same direction. Sliding the back foot behind the front foot, bend the back knee and shift the weight to the back foot, keeping the heel of the back foot down to stretch the achilles and lower part of the calf. Do not lock the knee. Hold. Repeat and then repeat to the opposite leg.

Calf Stretch

(This stretch can be done against a wall or with a partner.)

Place the feet in a comfortable stride position, *both feet* facing forward and weight on the back foot. Press the rear heel down to the floor with the back leg straight, but not locked. Hold.

b. To stretch the lower part of the calf and achilles, the same stretch may be used with the back leg bent and the heel still down. This stretch may be done one leg at a time (above-mentioned position) or both legs at the same time, as illustrated.

Foot Exercises

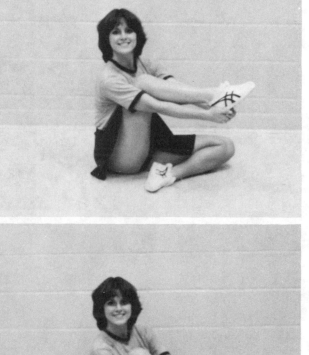

Wrist Exercises

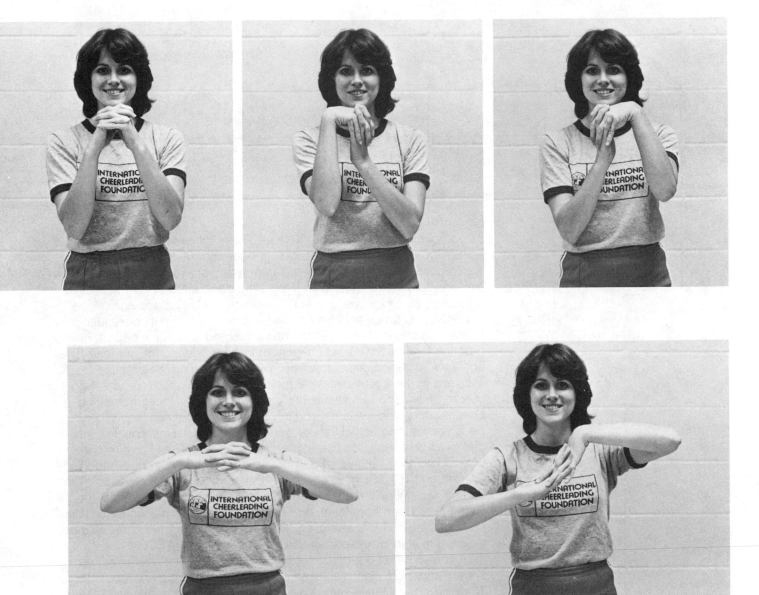

4

Tryouts

As you can probably imagine there are many different methods used across the country in the selection of cheerleaders. Since it would be impossible to list here all of the different types of tryouts, you should take it upon yourself to find out how tryouts are conducted at your school, who does the judging and exactly what you will be judged on.

To give you an idea, however, of what to expect, tryouts are usually held in the spring. This gives the newly elected squad the opportunity to practice together or attend cheerleading camp during the summer. The entire tryout period takes about two weeks, including the practice sessions or pre-tryout clinics. At the first pre-tryout session you will go over the rules and regulations of tryouts and you will meet the retiring cheerleaders who will teach you the cheers and routines that will be performed during actual tryouts. You may be given a citizenship form that must be completed by each of your teachers. (See Form A, page 56). You will also be given a permission form which must be signed by your parents (See Form B, page 57). This form will explain to your parents the duties the position involves, exactly what financial obligations are required from them, and other pertinent information regarding away games, summer camp, etc. Your parents or guardian may also be required to sign a medical release (See Form C, page 58).

During your first pre-tryout clinic you will begin learning one or two cheers and more than likely start on jumps and basic gymnastic stunts. Three or more of these sessions are usually held before tryouts. As you are learning the tryout material be sure to learn each movement correctly. Don't be embarrassed to ask questions. You must be confident when you are practicing on your own at home that you are performing the routine correctly.

Most schools have two tryout sessions: semifinals, which cut down or eliminate some of the candidates; and finals, during which the actual cheerleading squad is selected. During these tryouts you will be judged on your presentation of one or more cheers you learned during pre-tryout clinics. At some schools you will have to perform a cheer you, yourself, have made up. You may also be expected to perform a portion of a pompon routine and demonstrate jumps and gymnastic stunts. As we mentioned earlier, it depends entirely on the tryout system employed at your school as to what you will have to perform. In order to prepare you for any and everything, a sample judging form is shown: Read it carefully, and do note the various categories the judges score at the end of this chapter.

It goes without saying that you have to be fully prepared before you ever go to tryouts. You need to know how to practice the material you will be performing and exactly what to practice. The better you know the material, the more relaxed you will be, and your chances of being elected will be greater.

How to Practice and Prepare for Tryouts.

MAKE SURE YOU ARE IN GOOD PHYSICAL CONDITION FOR TRYOUTS. Cheerleaders are athletes and need to be aerobically fit. You will need endurance to enable you to cheer through an entire game, and you must be toned and strong to perform jumps, stunts, gymnastics, etc. Many times injuries happen DURING TRYOUTS due to a lack of conditioning. Read over the conditioning chapter in this book and set up a specific exercise routine for yourself.

ORGANIZE A PRACTICE SCHEDULE. List every tryout requirement and note the areas where you are strong and the areas where you are weak. Once this has been completed you can decide on how much practice time you will need to devote to each area. For example, if you have trouble with certain required gymnastics stunts, you will need to spend extra time on those skills. You might consider asking the school gymnastics coach for assistance or perhaps take a few lessons at a local gymnastics or dance school. Whatever you decide to do, you must begin working early so that you will be fully prepared at tryouts.

Practice Often and Consistently. Plan on practicing a half hour each day, rather than five hours in one day. The more you practice, the more you will build your confidence. If you have never been a cheerleader, your arm motions, jumps, pompon routines, etc., may look awkward and only lots of practice will change that! Imagine yourself as one of the judges. Would you select the candidate who looks uncomfortable and unsure of herself . . . or would you select the girl who performs each movement easily and naturally? If you really want to become a cheerleader, know your material and practice enough so that you can perform each requirement with ease.

Practice your routines with a friend to learn to cheer in unison. Watch yourself in a mirror. Practice your entire routine, from start to end, just as if you were going through tryouts in front of the judges.

Interviews. Sometimes interviews are required at tryouts to find out how well you present yourself to others, your speaking ability, and your self-confidence. Judges especially want to find out which candidates are serious about becoming cheerleaders and for what reasons. How can you prepare? Your interview will relate to cheerleading and school spirit so make sure you understand the real purpose of cheerleaders within a school. Know why you want to be a cheerleader. Practice in front of a mirror talking about your cheerleading goals, and be specific. Judges look for those candidates who are genuinely concerned about helping their school.

Teacher Evaluations. Teachers often are asked to provide information on candidates based on their behavior in the classroom. This data is scored and becomes part of your tryout score. Teachers note which candidates have proven themselves to be dependable, capable, coop- erative, prompt, and good students. Will your teachers have good things to say about you?

Visualize Your Tryout. Your mental preparation is important to your success. Picture the gymnasium, the judges, all the excited candidates, and YOURSELF! Are you confident? Do you have a sharp, cheerleader appearance (hair out of your face, clothes neat, smile on your face)? You're going to be nervous, naturally, which really will add to the excitement of tryouts, but never picture yourself worried. You must not be negative in any way. Are you wishing the others good luck? Your name is being called . . . are you slowly getting up and walking to your starting position or are you jumping up and running into place? Are you rushing through your cheers so you can hurry and get it over with or are you doing each movement thoroughly? You need to picture yourself doing a good job and enjoying every minute of it. The judges must feel that you love what you are doing and that you want to do your very best.

One more important thing to think about and remember. YOU MAKE A MISTAKE! Do you begin to cry, cover your face and run out of the gym? Do you get flustered and confused? Of course not! You smile, compose your thoughts, and continue on, if you can't continue, then begin over again—better than before!

To give you an overview of the important things to remember when you are trying out, use the following checklist:

1. **Warm Up Properly.** Avoid injuries at tryouts by stretching out before you perform.

2. **Execute Your Motions Smoothly.** Relax and avoid jerky, unnatural movements. Be careful not to speed up your cheers and skills. Take your time to do your routine just as you practiced at home.

3. **Project a Spirited Personality.** Don't overdo the enthusiasm or act "fakey," but an extra show of spirit will show the judges you are excited about cheerleading.

4. **Make Eye Contact with Individuals in the Crowd.** Pay attention to your audience. Move your eyes across the entire section of bleachers to show you are cheering for your audience. If you are thinking only about yourself, your eye contact will show it!

5. **Smile.** Show the judges you enjoy what you are doing.

6. **Project a Strong Voice.** Yell from your diaphram and make your voice natural and loud. Screaming or using a gruff voice is un-natural and offensive. Say your cheer words clearly so your audience can hear you.

7. **Show a Confident, Positive Attitude.** Believe in yourself. Hold your head up high and show the judges you are excited and determined.

8. **Be Poised.** If you are organized and have practiced thoroughly, it will show. And, should you forget part of your routine, so what! Don't fall apart, just let the judges know you are determined to do your routine. Smile, be confident, and begin again. Remember that a good cheerleader is poised and reacts well under stress.

9. **Know Why You Want to Be a Cheerleader.** If your goals are to help raise the pride and spirit in your school, it will be evident in the way you present yourself.

Shown below is a basic cheer for you to learn and begin practicing. Once you've learned the words and motions, pretend you are trying out, applying the important points mentioned above.

TRYOUT CHEER

"Fight"

"Ready"

"Eagles"

"Fight" (pause)

"Fight"

"Mighty"

→

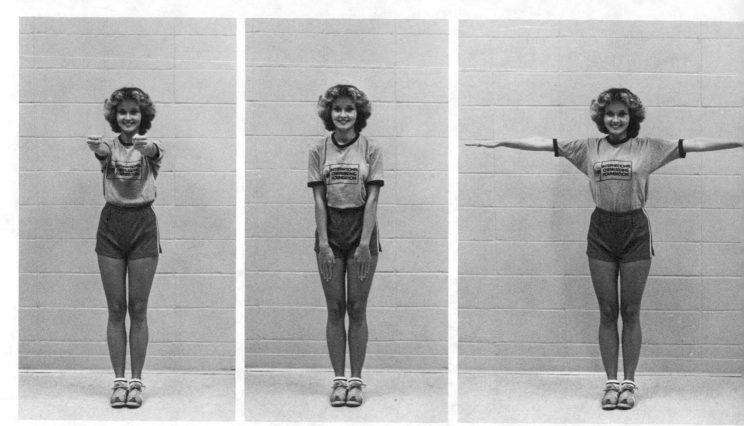

"Eagles"   (pause)   "Show 'em" →

"Fight"   "Mighty"   "Eagles" →

(pause)

"Your might"

(pause)

"Let's"

"Do it"

(pause)

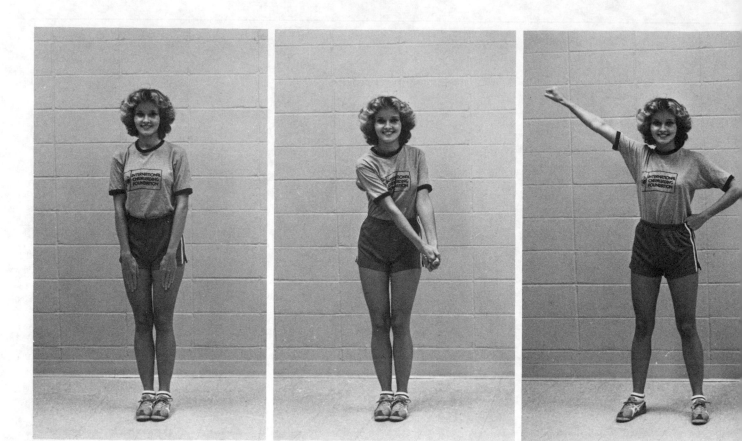

"Tonight"   (pause)   "Fight!"

SAMPLE GRADING/SCORING FORM
Cheerleader Tryouts

Item:	Poor (1)	Fair (2)	Good (3)	Superior (4)
PERSONALITY PROJECTION: Eye Contact, smile, sincerity, rapport with audience.	___	___	___	___
SPIRIT: Enthusiasm and ability to motivate the crowd.	___	___	___	___
CHEER MOTIONS: Sharp, strong, good placement.	___	___	___	___
TIMING AND RHYTHM: Routines balanced, flowing, smooth and natural.	___	___	___	___
APPEARANCE: Neatness, grooming.	___	___	___	___
VOICE PROJECTION: Loud, clear, natural.	___	___	___	___
JUMPS: Height, form, variety.	___	___	___	___
GYMNASTICS: Timing and technique.	___	___	___	___
DANCE ROUTINE: Dance ability and technique.	___	___	___	___
GROUP CHEER: Timing and unity with group.	___	___	___	___
OVERALL PERFORMANCE: Athletic ability, overall technique, and ability to motivate the crowd.	___	___	___	___
INTERVIEW ANSWERS:	___	___	___	___
TEACHER EVALUATION:	___	___	___	___

TOTALS: ___ ___ ___ ___

GRAND TOTAL: ___

FORM A

CITIZENSHIP FORM

The following form is an excellent example of the judgments that a student's teachers can make in offering information on how well a student might represent your school.

Name of Student _____   Class Subject: _____
Teacher: _____   Class Time (Days/Hour): _____

Profile Item:	Below Avg. (1)	Average (2)	Above Avg. (3)
a) Ability to Get Along with Others	_____	_____	_____
b) Attentiveness in Class	_____	_____	_____
c) Willingness to Help Classmates	_____	_____	_____
d) Quality of Work In and Out of Class	_____	_____	_____
e) Punctuality	_____	_____	_____
f) General Disposition	_____	_____	_____
g) Attendance Record	_____	_____	_____
h) General Grooming and Appearance	_____	_____	_____
i) Would This Person Represent Our School Well?	_____	_____	_____
TOTALS:	_____	_____	_____
GRAND TOTAL:	_____		

Note: This form should be given to the teachers of each cheerleader candidate. Upon completion, the forms are to be returned to the faculty cheerleader adviser, and should be considered totally confidential information, not to be shown to other teachers or students.

FORM B   **SAMPLE PARENTAL PERMISSION SLIP**

CHEERLEADER TRYOUTS

Dear Parent,

_____ has signified her desire to be a cheerleader at Franklin County High School. There are certain responsibilities and obligations which she must assume in order to remain a member of the F.C.H.S. squad.

Please notice the enclosed 1980–81 Cheerleader Constitution, where all rules and regulations are outlined. Won't you please read this constitution carefully before signing the form below?

A student receives many values from cheerleading and I sincerely hope that this experience will be an enriching and worthwhile one for your daughter.

_____
Cheerleader Sponsor, FCHS

_____ has my permission to participate as a member of the cheerleading squad at Franklin County High School. I have read the requirements established for all cheerleaders and I will assist in every way to see that they are enforced.

I understand that summer training will include required attendance at summer camp. This is in addition to the regular scheduled practices.

While I expect school authorities to exercise reasonable precaution to avoid injury, I understand that the school assumes no financial obligation for any injury that may occur.

This statement is to be for the school year 1980–81.

Parent: _____

Address: _____

Telephone: _____

Date: _____

FORM C

WAIVER FOR ATHLETIC INSURANCE

I understand one requirement of eligibility for athletic participation is adequate insurance coverage against injury while in practice or performance.

Since my son/daughter is adequately covered with such accident insurance policies which I already carry, I do not desire to obtain coverage under the standard DeKalb Insurance plan for athletics.

I have presented evidence to show my son/daughter is adequately with accident insurance and I request the requirement of coverage under the school athletic insurance plan be waived.

I hereby state I am the legal guardian of said child and I am authorized to make this decision.

_____   _____
(Insurance Co. and Policy #)   (Signature of Parent)

_____   _____
(date)   (Signature of Student)

_____

MEDICAL RELEASE FORM

I, _____, do hereby release Gadsden High School, sponsors and administrators, from responsibility in case of illness or injury of my child, _____, while performing her cheerleading duties (this includes travel and clinic).

I also give permission for treatment of illness and injury that may be sustained while performing said duties.

_____   _____
(name of doctor)   (signature of parent of guardian)

_____   _____
(Insurance Co. and Policy #)   (date)

5

Cheers

A cheer is an organization and coordination of words and motions, with a designated beginning and ending, relating to an athletic event. While *chants* are used continually throughout a game, *cheers* are used only when play has been stopped on the field or court. At this time, all eyes are on the cheerleader and your cheers should highlight the crowd's support of the team.

There Are as Many Different Cheer Styles as There Are Cheerleading Squads. Every squad has its own unique style ranging from precision movements (which involve strict timing and sharp, definite motions) to flowing, dance-like movements. It is not uncommon for a squad to combine these two styles to create an even more unique style of its own. One example is the blending of precision arm motions with bouncing feet motions. Do remember that every squad will eventually develop its own special style of performing a cheer.

The Purpose of a Cheer Is to Draw a Unified Response from Your Crowd. Your athletes will be more inspired hearing an entire crowd shouting their support together, than hearing each fan cheering by himself. Keep in mind that cheers should be easy to follow, as your crowd will not respond to tongue-tangling words and small, intricate motions.

A Cheer Is Usually Presented During an Official Break in an Athletic Event. Official breaks include time-outs, change of quarters, half-time, etc. Cheers can also be performed before and after games. All of your cheers should be prepared in advance and should cover all possible game situations.

Organization Is the Key to Performing Effective Cheers. You should know ahead of time what cheers you will be using and under what game condition they will be used. An effective squad is aware of the progress of the game and wastes no time beginning an appropriate cheer when an official break is called. Do remember that breaks vary in length, so be sure you know how long time-outs, quarter changes, etc., are so that you will have adequate time to perform your cheers.

Now That You Know the Definition and Purpose of a Cheer, You Should Know How to Learn One. Since there are so many cheers with different meanings, it is important that you learn and know the words. Your team isn't watching you during a game, they are listening to you. Therefore, the only way you and your crowd can show support is through the words of your cheers. You must not only *know* the words, you must know how to properly *project* the words so that your crowd can follow them and yell with you.

When you are learning and practicing words, be sure that you enunciate well and that you project each word clearly and strongly. You need to learn to project your normal voice from your diaphragm. Do not force yourself and do not yell gruffly. NEVER scream. Incorrect voice control and yelling can damage your vocal cords. To practice proper voice projection, place your hands on your stomach just below your ribs. Say the word "hey" in your normal voice. Now project the word "hey" from your diaphragm. If you are projecting correctly, you will feel your ribs contract as your diaphragm pushes the word out.

Once you have learned the words to your cheer, and how to project them, you begin learning the arm and feet motions. Start with the first three or four motions and practice them several times. When you have learned these motions, practice the next three or four motions, adding them to those you have already learned. Continue this procedure until you have learned the entire cheer. Watch yourself in a mirror to make sure that your motions are perfectly placed and executed. Be sure to say the words each time you practice a motion so that the entire cheer will begin to flow together. Don't get frustrated if you forget a motion or some of the words. You've just learned something new and you will have to practice many times before the cheer becomes natural.

The final step to learning a cheer is adding your own personality. When you practice, ALWAYS add a smile and an excited, spirited expression. If you practice with personality, you will perform with personality.

Since the only effective way to perfect your cheers is through practice, you will undoubtedly develop your own methods of learning and perfecting. You should, however, begin practicing in front of a mirror and then have someone watch you and constructively criticize your mistakes. Once you've become a cheerleader and begin practicing with your squad, your adviser will attend practice and offer constructive criticism and suggestions. You must *want* to be criticized on your mistakes so you can work toward perfecting your cheers.

It is a good idea to occasionally practice in a different location. You don't want to be confused the first time you do a cheer in different surroundings. You might want to practice in a public area, such as a park, to get used to performing in front of people.

Basic Styles and Motions. Although there are many different styles used by cheerleaders across the nation, all motions originate from the standard basic motions. Practice the nine basic motions on the following pages. Watch yourself in a mirror as you work on the exact position of your arms and legs, and go over each motion until it is perfect. You can work on your timing and rhythm as you practice the cheers at the end of the chapter. Keep in mind these important tips:

1. Keep your head up.
2. Smile.
3. Don't stare at one point.
4. Make the motion sharp and peppy.
5. Check to see if you are doing the motion exactly right (for example, is your hand supposed to be open or in a closed fist?).

BASIC MOTIONS

Basic Arm Motions

Daggers   Vertical-Up   High "V"

Horizontal

Low "V"

Vertical-Down

Hands on Hips

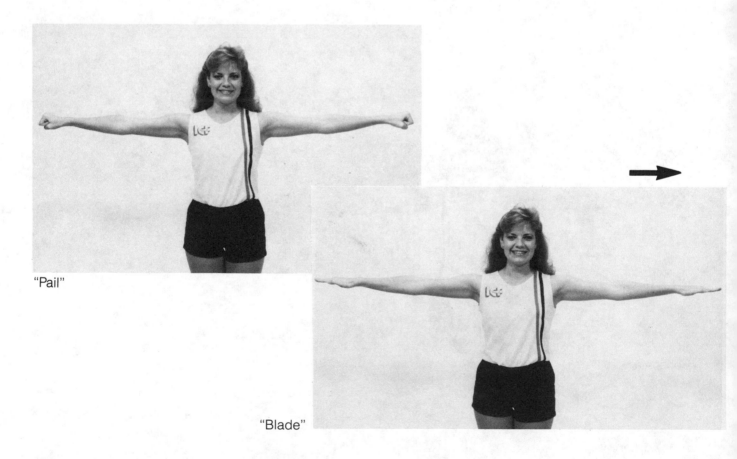

"Pail"

"Blade"

Punch

Diagonal

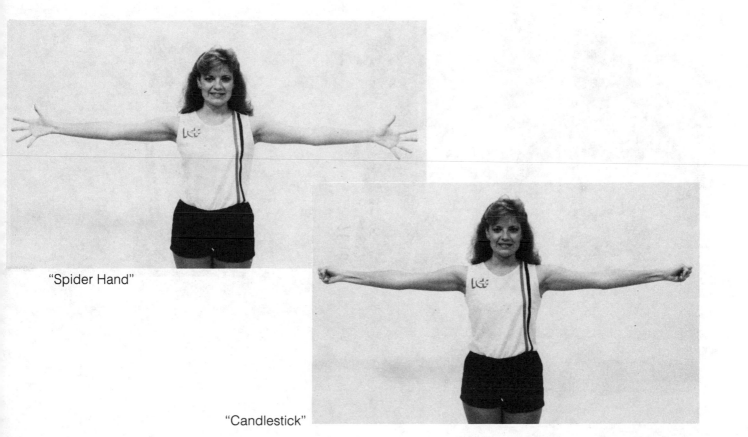

"Spider Hand"

"Candlestick"

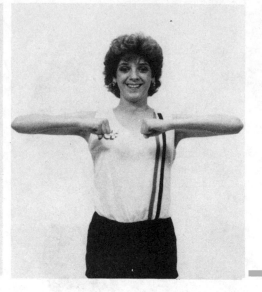

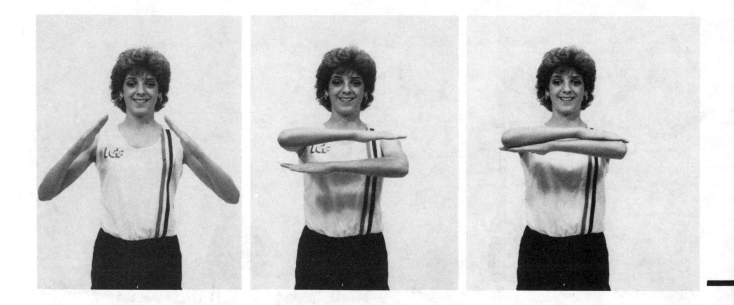

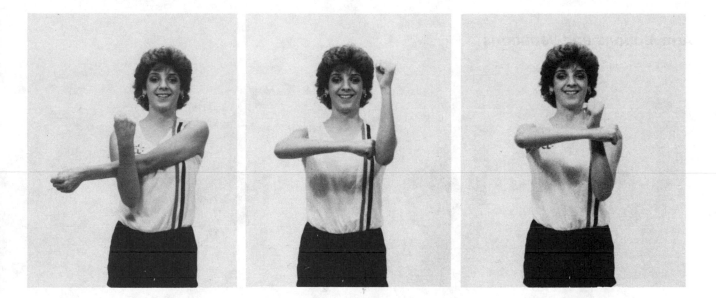

Arm Motions and Variations   Vertical-Up

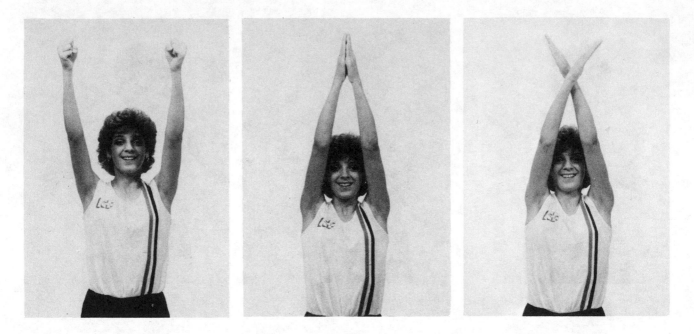

Arm Motions and Variations   High "V"

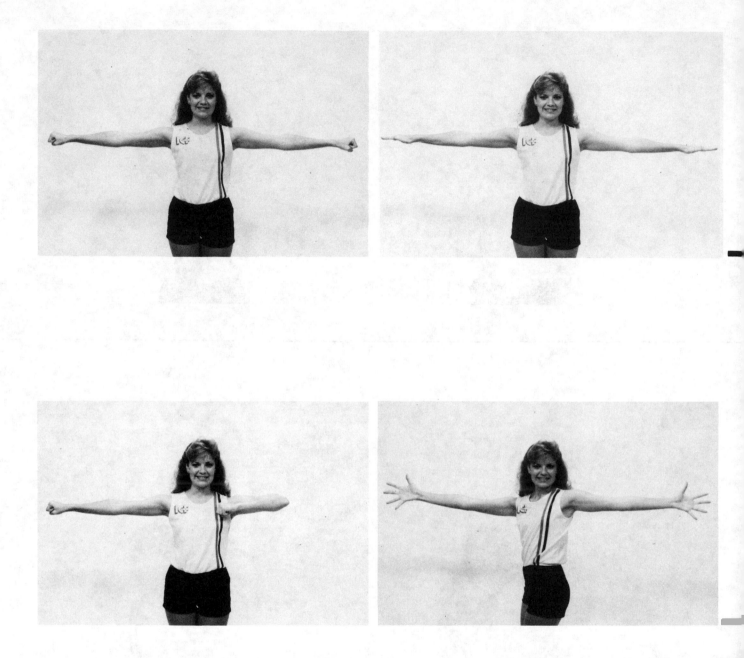

Arm Motions and Variations

Low "V"

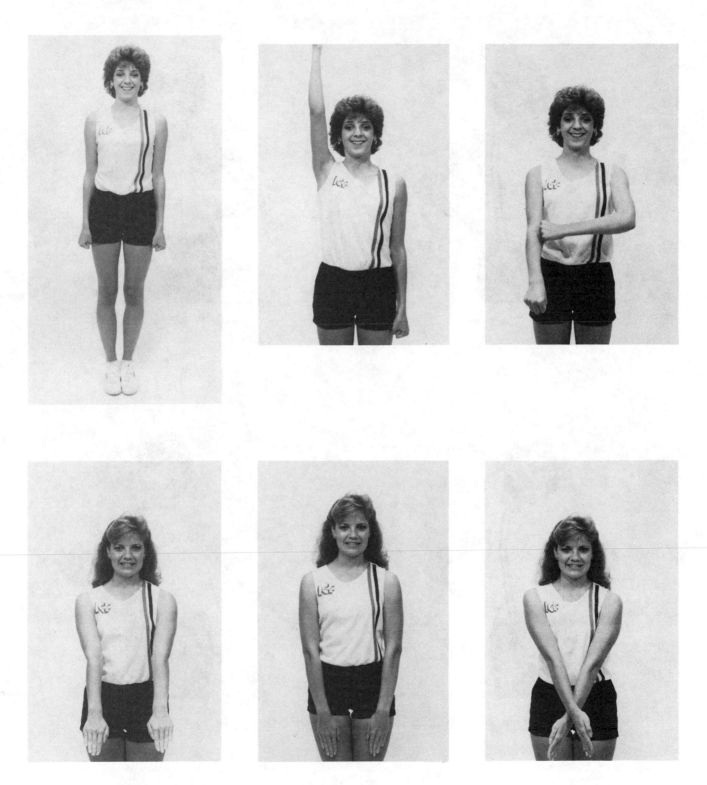

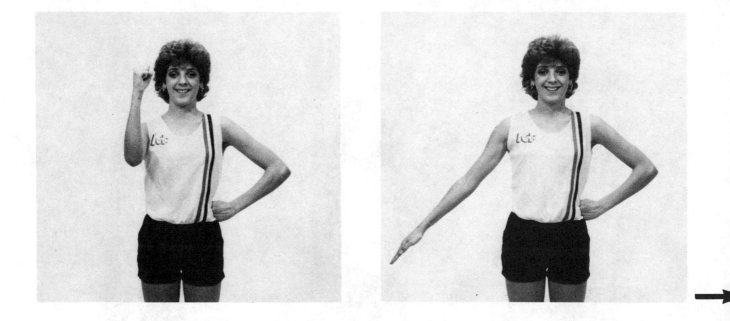

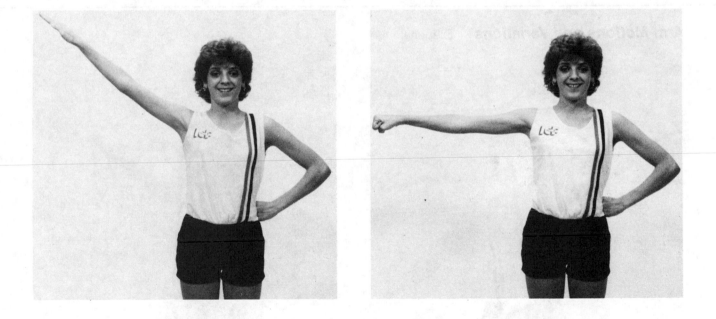

Arm Motions and Variations
Punch

Arm Motions and Variations Diagonal

Arm Motions and Variations—Common Mistakes

The most common arm motion mistake is flying arms (when arms are extended horizontally, they are either up too high or back too far). To avoid this, flex your shoulders and think "extension from shoulder level," instead of eye level.

Other common mistakes made in cheer motions are pictured below, with tips on how to correct them.

MISTAKE: turned-up wrists
CORRECTION: pull down and straighten

MISTAKE: turned-down
wrists
CORRECTION: pull down
and straighten

MISTAKE: flying arms, too high
CORRECTION: pull down
to shoulder level

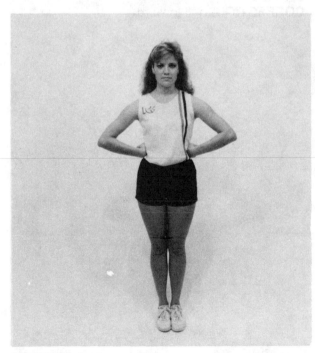

MISTAKE: broken wrists,
forward
CORRECTION: pull back
and straighten

MISTAKE: broken wrists,
down, and fingers apart
CORRECTION: pull up and
straighten, with fingers together

MISTAKE: broken wrists, down
CORRECTION: pull up and straighten

MISTAKE: flying arms, back too far
CORRECTION: pull forward

MISTAKE: palms forward
CORRECTION: turn palms in or out

MISTAKE: turned-up wrists
CORRECTION: pull up to straighten

MISTAKE: chin down, arms not straight
CORRECTION: pull chin up and straighten arms

MISTAKE: lopsided "V"
CORRECTION: even up arms

Adding Personality . . . what's wrong in these pictures?

No Expression

Weak Smile

Unconvincing

Just Right

Too Much

"Fakey"

Leg Positions

SAMPLE CHEERS

Basic Arm Motion Cheer—"Command"

"Ready"

(Pause)

"Get"

(Clap)

Eagles

"Take"

"Over"　　　　　　　"It"　　　　　　　(Clap)

"Command"　　　　　　　(Jump)　　　　　　　"Back"

(slap) You'll   "See"   (Pause)

"Rise"

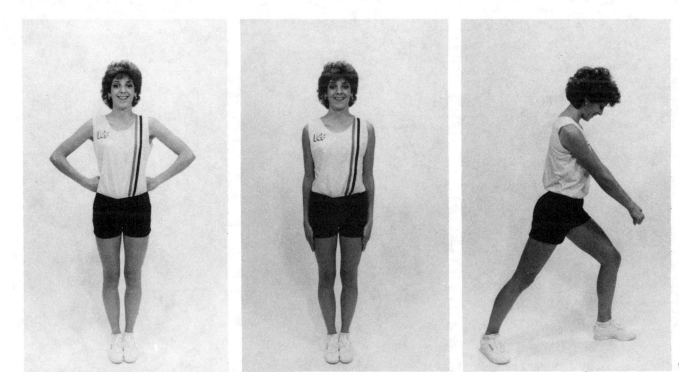

"Ready—O.K."   (Pause)   "Eagle"

"Eagle"   "territo—"   "ry!"

"Team will"   "Rise"   (Pause)   →

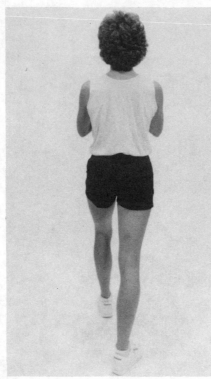

"Take you"

"By Sur—"

"prise!"

"Course"

(Pause)

(Pause)

"We're on"

"Our Winning"

"Eagle"

"Fear the"

"Force!"

Chapter Summary

- A cheer is an organization and coordination of words and motions, with a designated beginning and ending, relating to an athletic event.
- Styles of cheering vary with each squad. They range from precision to dance-like movements.
- Cheers draw unified responses from the crowd.
- Cheers should be performed before and after games and during official breaks.
- Organization is the key to an effective cheer performance.
- You learn a cheer by knowing the words first, and then the arm and foot motions. Segment learning is the most effective method of learning an entire cheer, with constant practice in front of a mirror.
- Practice by yourself and then in front of someone.
- Practice makes perfect!

Hints and Advice on Performing a Cheer

- Cheer with your head up (it shows confidence).
- Facial expressions reflect enthusiasm and excitement, so smile constantly.
- Arm placement should be exact.
- Yell from your diaphragm for strong, clear voice projection.
- Maintain good eye contact with your crowd.
- Enter and exit from the court or field with enthusiasm. Spirit is usually continuous throughout a game and a cheer, if performed well from start to finish, will highlight this spirit.

6

Chants

A chant is an organization and coordination of words and motions, performed spontaneously throughout an athletic event, to generate crowd spirit and support. Chants, often referred to as "side-line chants" or "sidelines," are repeated several times.

Chants, Like Cheers, Vary from Coast to Coast. An experienced cheerleader realizes the importance of the use of many different types of chants. Performing a variety of styles will enable you to capture and hold your crowd's attention, while use of only one style can often become monotonous. Imagine a cheerleader executing a perfect toe-touch jump. Now imagine her doing that same jump at every exciting moment in the game. After several repetitions, it begins to lose some of its effect and becomes "old hat."

This simple example illustrates the need for variety. In fact, variety is necessary in every single area of cheerleading, whether it be jumps, cheers, chants or stunts.

Chants Are Closely Related to Cheers as They Are Both Combinations of Words and Actions. Precision movements and dance-like styles can be incorporated into your chants, but many are simply accompanied by claps, stomps or snaps. Unlike cheers, which are performed only during official breaks and before or after games, chants are performed *during* games. They may, of course, be used in place of cheers, but their most important function is during the actual game play.

The Purpose of a Chant Is to Help You Keep the Spirit and Energy Level of Your Crowd Up Throughout the Game. It is important, therefore, that you practice your chants in such a manner that their performance comes easily to you. In fact, they should become second nature to you. Since they are performed spontaneously, you must have a wide reperetoire that covers every single game situation. This means, of course, that you should have a thorough knowledge of each sport you cheer for so that you will know what chant is appropriate in a particular situation.

The three main types of chants you will use are: 1) chants that your crowd yells along with; 2) chants that the crowd will repeat after you, and; 3) crowd competition yells (where one section of the crowd will compete against another section in yelling). The motions for your chants are the same you use in your cheers (refer to Chapter 5).

When Learning and Practicing Chants You Should Pretend You Are Actually Cheering at a Game. You should practice in this manner: 1) repeat the chant several times so that you are familiar with the words; 2) repeat three or four different chants in succession; 3) give a "one more time" signal and practice cutting off a chant. To help you quickly initiate chants, write down different game situations (jump ball, touchdown, free throw, etc.). Put them into a container and then select one. Begin immediately performing as many chants as you know that relate to that particular game situation. Remember when practicing chants to project your words and to add personality. Be sure to have someone watch you and offer constructive criticism on how you can improve.

Begin practicing the sample chants we have pictured in the following pages, and be sure to study the list of important hints at the end of the chapter.

SAMPLE CHANTS

"G-O, GO!"

"Ready—O.K. . . . G"

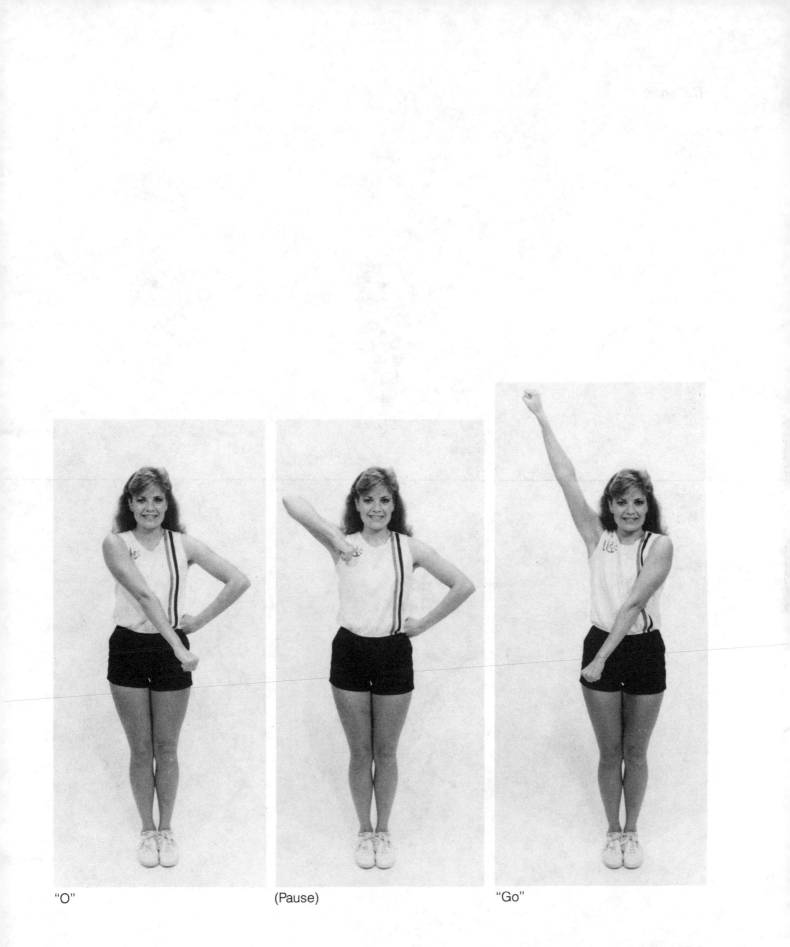

"O"   (Pause)   "Go"

Defense

(Pause)   "Let's"

"We're Fired Up"

"We're   "Fired"

"Go!"

"Up! We're"   "Sizzlin"   "in! We"

"Can't"   "Be"   "Stopped!"   (Repeat)

Chapter Summary

- A chant is an organization and coordination of words and motions, performed spontaneously throughout an athletic event, to generate crowd spirit and support.
- Variety is a necessity.
- Chants can be performed before or after a game, but are more importantly used *during* games.
- You should have a surplus of chants that will cover any game situation.
- Practice chants by pretending you are actually cheering at a game.

Hints and Advice on Performing Chants

- Start chants at a slow tempo
- Enunciate and put expression into your words.
- Vary your rhythms and styles.
- Chant motions should be as unified as cheer motions.
- Never use chants that are intended to insult the opposing team or an official.
- Continually incorporate new chants.

(Note: Hints for cheers can also be applied to chants. See Chapter 5.)

7

Jumps

Your primary role as a cheerleader is to keep your crowd interested and spirited—and nothing is more eye-catching than a well-executed jump. Any advanced cheerleader will tell you that performing good jumps is one of the most important abilities a cheerleader should possess.

Jumps are used continuously throughout games because they are exciting to watch, can be executed quickly in a limited space, and look difficult to the ordinary sports spectator. Since they are impressive and interesting to watch, they will do much to gain the respect of your crowd. In addition, the spirit and enthusiasm they represent will help establish a line of communication between you and your crowd.

Jumps can be used in any of the following game situations:

1. before, during, or after cheers and chants
b. as part of a fight song or dance routine
3. during player introductions
4. following exciting plays
5. in combination with gymnastic tricks

Jumps should never be used in negative situations, such as opposing players fouling out or being injured.

You should use a variety of jumps throughout a game, as they are used more often than other cheerleading skills. In addition to the standard jumps pictured in this chapter, emphasis should be placed on the use of combination jumps and unique jumps or arm positions, as they are especially effective in gaining your crowd's attention.

A great deal of energy and skill is needed for jumping, so proper preparation is a must. Although some people have natural jumping ability, more often than not, the skill has to be learned and practiced regularly. Before you can even begin practicing the different types of jumps, you must be thoroughly warmed up. Start with the basic exercises pictured in chapter 3, and add the following:

1) Stand in place and jump straight up and down ten times. Next, do the same ten jumps on your right leg, then on your left leg. Continue this exercise, decreasing each time the number of times you jump on each foot (10, then 9, then 8, etc.). Remember to flex your knees as you land and rebound.

2) Practice kicking as high as possible, keeping your legs and back straight. Start with low to medium kicks and work up to your highest. Remember as you are doing this exercise to point your toes and keep your chin up.

3) Stand behind a chair and hold on to the top of it. As you hold, bend your knees, press down, and jump off the floor, spreading your legs as far apart as possible. This exercise can also be done with a partner—who takes the place of the chair by bending at the waist and grasping her knees—and is particularly good for helping you extend on the spread eagle, split, and herkie jumps.

4) Practice your approach for both single and combination jumps by doing a "pyramid" of straight jumps. Begin with a single straight jump, then a double, a triple . . . up to ten. Then reverse the order going to 9, 8, 7 . . . back down to a single jump. Emphasize use of the arms and correct timing of arms and legs.

These exercises will limber you up and prepare you for more advanced jumps. Work on them consistently, as they will firm your leg muscles, improve your spring, develop good coordination of arms and legs, and make your kicks straighter and higher.

Proper execution of a jump includes good height and correct form. Both aspects of jumping should be practiced separately before beginning actual jumps.

Correct form is the result of proper arm and leg position during a jump. The positioning of the body can be learned most easily by assuming the final jump position on the ground. From here you should try to feel and "memorize" with your muscles and joints the proper form.

Arm motions are extremely important to the form of a jump because they help you to gain upward lift, height, and momentum. Since the use of your arms is instrumental in achieving both height and form—the keys to a good jump—you must spend time practicing them. Stand in front of a mirror and decide where you want your arms to be when you are at the top of a jump. As you watch yourself, be sure that your arms are correctly placed.

Your legs are also important in a jump. In most jumps they must be straight. Practice standing on one foot and extending the other straight out, pointing your toes. Tighten the muscles in one leg, and then lift that leg off the ground. These exercises will show you how your legs should look and feel during a jump, and will help you keep your legs straight.

One other way to practice good form is to break a jump down into its individual parts. After you determine what each body part does in a jump, practice them separately. Gradually add each body part together until you have a complete jump. This is helpful for learning the more advanced and unique jumps.

Developing good height in jumps requires a lot of dedicated practice. The following exercises are very helpful for achieving maximum height in your jumps.

1) Jump onto box. Select a sturdy "box" (any elevated surface, approximately 6–12 inches, in a safe area will do). Using your normal approach, jump up onto the "box" ten times; repeat this 3 times. Gradu-

ally increase the height of your "box" as your jumps get higher.

2) Jump off box.   Again, select a sturdy "box" in a safe area. This time step off the "box" rebound from both feet and execute your practice jump. Repeat 10 times for each jump. Increase the height of your "box" as you progress in jumping ability.

3) Lunges   Stand with both feet together. Step out into a deep lunge (be sure to keep your knee over the front toes and your back leg straight), drive with the front leg to the standing position on one foot, step out with the opposite foot, and repeat. Complete 12 consecutive steps, alternating legs. Repeat 3 times. Start with your own body weight and either add small hand weights or lunge up an incline as you get stronger.

You are now ready to learn a jump. Keep in mind that there are three equally important steps to any jump: 1) the approach or beginning; 2) the jump itself, and; 3) the ending. You should decide on what jump you are going to do and what arm motion you are going to add. Determine also your approach and ending.

There are quite a number of different approaches used by cheerleaders, but the standard approach is pictured at the beginning of our jump illustrations in this chapter. No matter what approach you use, be sure to give your jump momentum and height. Remember that what you do with your arms during your approach is as important as what you do with your legs. Your timing must be coordinated. Make it a rule to hold your head high while you are jumping, as this will make your jump appear two to three inches higher.

On your ending, you need to remember never to land with your knees stiff. Keep your knees flexed as you come down so they can absorb your weight. Be most careful not to land flat-footed or straight-legged. At the end of a jump your arms should never be dangling.

As you jump, work on your facial expression. You should never have a strained expression. Concentrate on smiling and looking confident. Make your jump look easy . . . if you show any discomfort in your face, your audience will certainly notice.

The following pictures show the approach, basic jumps and variations, as well as a sample cheer utilizing a jump. Practice carefully, warm up adequately, and don't forget to smile! Be sure to read the helpful hints on jumps at the end of the chapter.

Tuck Jump

"C" Jump

Spread Jump

Herkie Jump

Stag Jump

Toe Touch with Variations

Split

Hurdler

Pike

Double-9

Double Jumps

→

Hints and Advice on Performing Jumps

- Warm up thoroughly.
- Decide on which jump, arm motion, approach and ending you will use.
- Make sure your arm motions give momentum and height.
- Coordinate the timing of your arms and legs.
- Keep your knees flexed as you land.
- Make the jump look easy, hold your head high and smile.
- If jumps are used simultaneously in a squad cheer, make sure that each cheerleader uses the same approach and that form and height are uniform.
- Vary your jumps, but only use those you have perfected.
- Practice regularly.

8

Gymnastics

Gymnastics have become an extremely exciting, impressive sport. Consequently, cheerleading has benefited from the sport's growth. Gymnastic skills help cheerleaders to develop a higher spirit level through innovative crowd motivation.

A good cheerleader can creatively incorporate gymnastics into routines. A gymnastic skill must work smoothly into a cheer. If you just "stick it in" it will look awkward and out of place. Here are a few examples of where gymnastics can be appropriately, and smoothly, used:

1. to begin a cheer
2. to end a cheer
3. to correspond with the words of a cheer (roll over you, etc.)
4. when your players are being introduced at the beginning of the game
5. when your team scores
6. in coordination with a pyramid or series of stunts
7. in a pompon routine

The gymnastics you incorporate into your routines should be snappy and peppy, not slow and controlled. Therefore, the use of a back handspring or a cartwheel is much more appropriate than a front limber. By using combinations of various skills performed by pairs or groups, beginner as well as advanced skills can be extremely effective.

Before you begin learning actual gymnastic skills, work on the flexibility stretches shown in this chapter, as well as the basic exercises shown in Chapter 3. These will help you to develop the necessary flexibility, control and strength. Remember to stretch your muscles . . . don't force them.

GYMNASTIC EXERCISES

Partner Straddle-Stretch

Hints:

- back straight
- knees locked
- head up
- knees pointing straight up

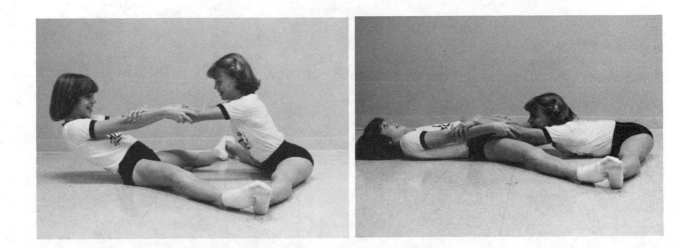

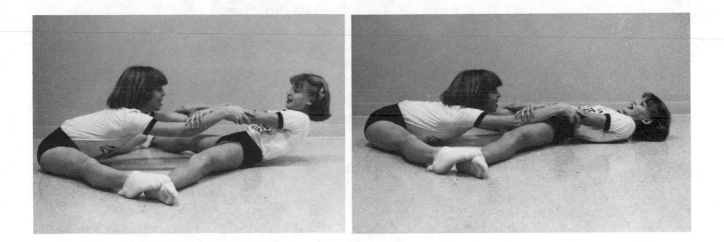

Partner Leg Stretch

Hints:

- leg locked
- top pointed
- hips flat against wall

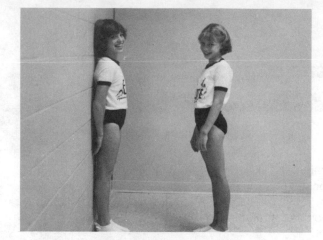

Bridge

Hints:

- feet flat
- hands by ears, elbows up

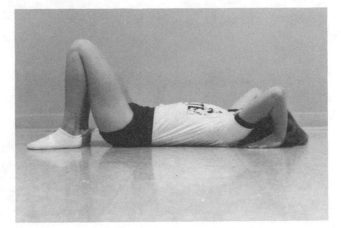

- arms straight

- knee up, hold, alternate legs

- straighten leg, hold, alternate legs

- walk feet out to straighten legs

Back Limber

Hints:

- reach up and back with arms and head
- extend legs to lift hips up

Before you begin practicing the beginning gymnastic skills we have pictured in this chapter, you should know that it often takes specialized training to successfully perform gymnastics. Advanced gymnastics, in particular, require a coach who can not only spot, but can detect your mistakes and correct them.

The following pictures show the basic skills in the beginning, intermediate and advanced levels of gymnastics (as they pertain to cheerleading). Variations to endings have been included to add creativity.

Remember that you should always have a spotter when you are learning a new gymnastic skill until you are absolutely confident that you have mastered the skill. A spotter is a person who helps you to learn a skill by holding and guiding you through it. Your spotter should not be afraid to "maintain contact with you as you attempt the skill and should, under no circumstances, let go of you. In other words, your spotter should see you through the skill, from start to finish safely. Remember that injuries are usually the result of "clowning around" or attempting a skill that is too advanced.

You will notice that we have purposely deleted spotting techniques for the pictures of advanced gymnastic skills. Anyone desiring to learn these advanced skills should seek help from a competent coach.

Be sure to read the helpful hints at the end of the chapter, and don't forget to warm up!

GYMNASTICS

Splits

Hints:

- lock front leg (front knee up; back knee down)
- hips squared
- do not bounce—stretch!
- shoulders back
- keep back leg bent (only if necessary)

Getting in and out of the Split

Hints:

- legs straight, knees locked
- hips squared; front knee up, back knee down
- press up, shoulders over hands
- lift hips

Forward Roll

Hints:

- reach forward
- place back of neck (not top of head) on floor
- keep elbows in
- maintain tight tuck

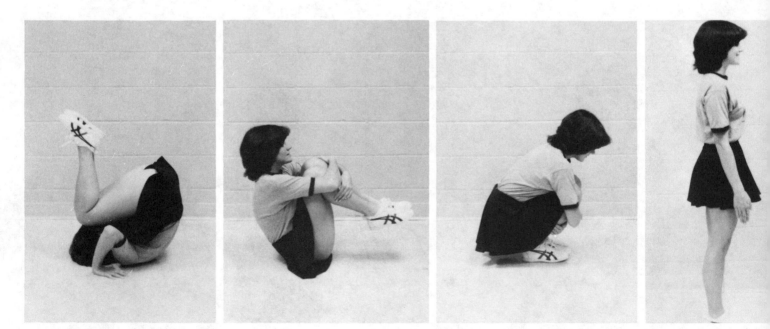

Side Roll

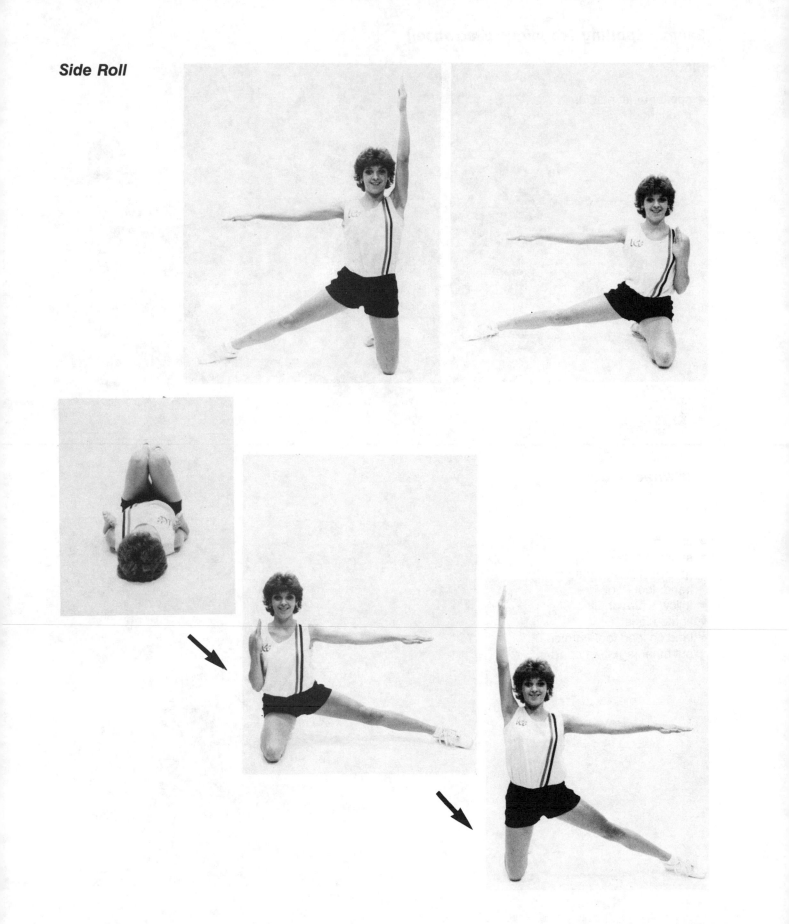

Sample Spotting Technique (Cartwheel)

Hint:

• spotter must hold on
  throughout

Cartwheel

Hints:

• stretch up
• reach to side
• rhythm (1-2-3-4) hands,
  hand, foot, foot
• follow a straight line
• tighten legs
• land on lead foot (stretch
  out other leg), feet apart

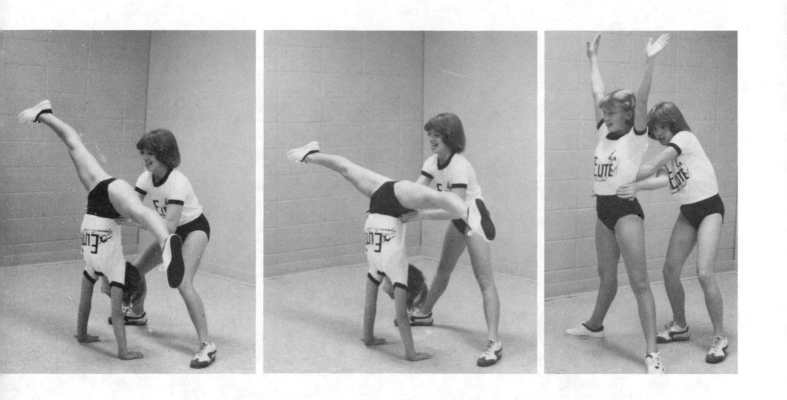

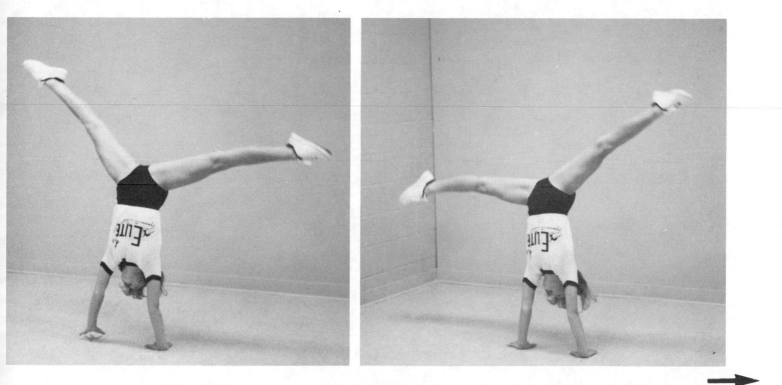

Dive Cartwheel

Hints:

- requires spotter
- step, swing arm back and shoot forward
- land on hands
- continue and finish same as cartwheel

One-Hand Cartwheel

Hints:

- requires spotter
- swing lead hand past floor and out to side
- proceed same as cartwheel

Front Limber

Hints:

- requires spotter
- kick to handstand (shoulders, hips, knees and ankles form straight line)
- to stand: press heels down, roll knees forward, followed by hips and chest; head is the last to come up

Front Walkover

Hints:

- kick up onto hands, legs remain split
- keep head back
- touch lead foot on floor, use other one as if trying to take a giant step
- foot drive is important (heel drive)
- let body roll up
- keep head back to return to standing position
- requires spotter

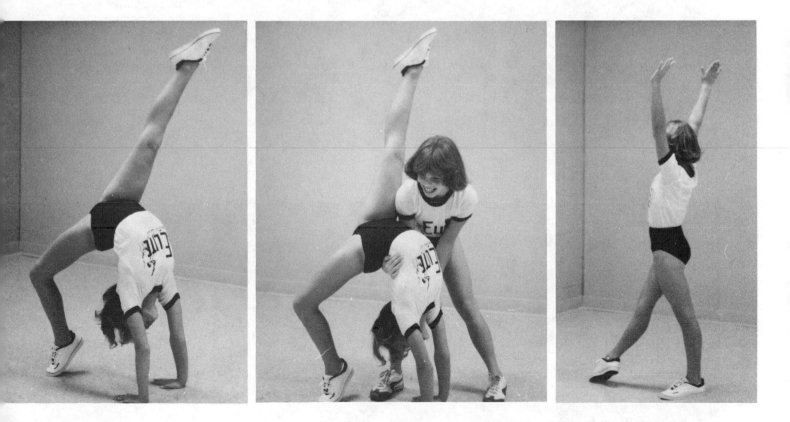

Switch-Leg Front Walkover (By pass)

Hints:

- requires spotter
- same procedure as front walkover; legs switch at handstand from split to one leg to split on the other

One-Handed Front Walkover

Hints:

- requires spotter
- place one hand down, swing other one past floor and up
- proceed as in walkover

Partner Walkover

Hints:

- requires two spotters
- procedure same as in one-handed front walkover
- partners hold forearms

Tinsica

Hints:

- requires spotter
- procedure same as in front walkover
- displace hands, one in front of the other

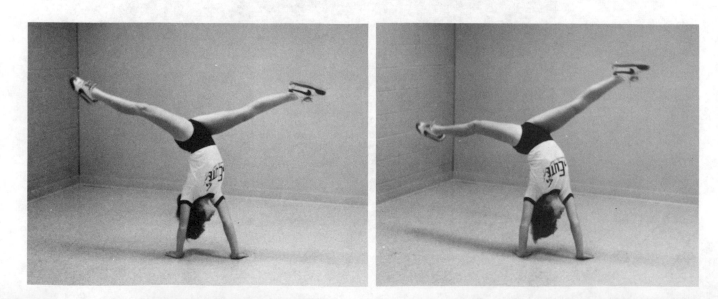

Back Walkover

Hints:

- requires spotter
- all weight on back leg; front toe just touching floor
- stretch up, then reach back
- front leg will drive to floor
- keep head back to help pull legs over
- lock arms
- extend throughout the skill (straight legs, arms, stretched torso, etc.)

Back Walkover to Knee-Sit

Hints:

- requires spotter
- begin same as back walkover
- bring legs together at handstand position
- tuck knees and place on floor (with control)

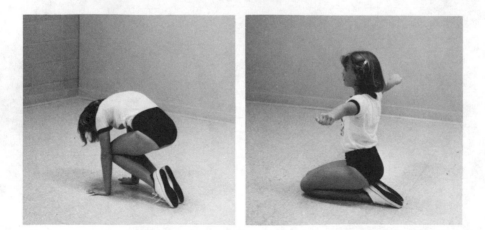

Back Walkover Splice

Hints:

- requires spotter
- procedure same as in back walkover
- when lead foot touches floor, press body up at shoulders, slide lead foot through the split

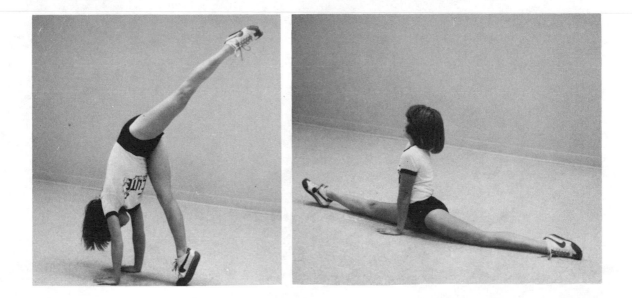

Front Handspring

Seek the assistance of a qualified gymnastic or acrobatic coach when attempting this.

Back Handspring

Seek the assistance of a qualified gymnastic or acrobatic coach when attempting this.

Back Handspring from Forward Roll

Seek the assistance of a qualified gymnastic or acrobatic coach when attempting this.

Aerial Cartwheel

Seek the assistance of a qualified gymnastic or acrobatic coach when attempting this.

Aerial Front Walkover

Seek the assistance of a qualified gymnastic or acrobatic coach when attempting this.

Hints and Advice on Performing Gymnastic Skills

- Warm up.
- Think of safety.
- Always have a spotter with you until you have mastered a skill.
- Start with beginning skills; master these, then move on.
- Good form means good extension and control.
- Any gymnastics used in cheerleading should be organized and skillfully incorporated into routines.
- If your squad uses gymnastics, see that no one person is singled out because of her gymnastics talent or lack of it.
- During a game use only the skills you have mastered, do not attempt skills you are unsure of.
- Gymnastics are meant to add to the excitement of your cheerleading, not to distract the crowd from the game.
- Practice gymnastics regularly.
- Utilize all ability levels.
- Beware of surfaces on which you are tumbling, i.e., hardwood floors, mats, grass.
- Combine difficult and simple skills that complement each other.
Incorporating stunts using pairs or groups is effective.
- Proper technique is essential.

9

Double Stunts

Cheerleading squads across America include double stunts in their repertoire of cheering skills. Double stunts, also referred to as partner stunts or simply stunts, are relatively simple when executed properly, but look difficult and spectacular to your crowd. They are easily incorporated into routines and add versatility to any performance.

Two people work together to build a double stunt. The "base" lifts and holds the "mounter." A "spotter" should also be involved when you are learning and practicing a new stunt. Use the spotter until the stunt is perfected.

INCORPORATION. Stunts can be used in cheers, exciting game situations, or anytime to generate spirit. Smooth incorporation is necessary for stunts to be effective. If you use them in your cheers, whether at the beginning, middle, or end, be sure they fit smoothly into the rhythm of the cheer. Since a stunt is a partner activity and takes several seconds to build, don't be caught building a stunt if a situation calls for a quick display of spirit; use a jump or gymnastic instead. Remember, incorporation of a stunt also includes a precise, enthusiastic dismount.

TECHNIQUE. Although co-ed squads (male-female) usually perform advanced, high-extension double stunts, the majority of stunts can be performed by two girls. Knowing the proper technique is the key to safe, successful stunts. Timing and balance are also important. Some of the more advanced stunts require a certain degree of power and strength, but these are usually performed by co-ed squads or very experienced cheerleaders.

HOW TO LEARN A DOUBLE STUNT. Every stunt, no matter how easy or difficult, will take time to polish and perfect. As you begin to learn, start with the easier stunts and work your way up. As you gain confidence and skill, progress to the more advanced stunts.

Before attempting any stunt, follow these important rules:

1. Be sure your body is completely warmed up.
2. Use at least one spotter.
3. Know the mounting and dismounting responsibilities of the mounter, base, and spotter.

Everyone must give her total concentration and effort to safely learn a stunt. Preventing accidents or injuries is everyone's responsibility. Never clown around while working on a stunt. This means no talking unless it pertains to the stunt. If there is any problem while attempting the stunt, be prepared to say the word "DOWN." This signals the mounter to immediately dismount.

THE BASE. Study the exact position of the base in the photographs throughout this chapter. Your body position is crucial to the mounter's (and the base's) safety! Center your weight through the midline of your body and keep your feet flat. Stay firm and balanced at all times. Never watch your mounter unless it is necessary in building. If you must look at your mounter, glance quickly; otherwise, watch your audience at all times. Remain poised with a pleasant look on your face no matter how strenuous the stunt.

THE MOUNTER. Tight body control is a must. Always use the "step-lock" climbing technique and distribute your weight as evenly as possible. Keep your shoulders squared, your mid-section pulled up, and your head up. Know your arm placement once you have built the stunt. When climbing or jumping onto your base, always press straight down;

PARTNER STUNTS

Pony Mount

BASE: Stand with feet shoulder width apart; knees slightly bent; hands on thighs, above knees; arms locked; back flat; head up.
MOUNTER: Stand DIRECTLY behind base; place one hand on lower back, other hand on shoulder for support.

NEVER pull or push your base off balance. Finally, eye contact and facial expression are important to make the stunt attractive to your audience.

SPOTTING A DOUBLE STUNT. A spotter's job is to catch the mounter in the event of a fall. A spotter may also stabilize the stunt as it is attempted but do not try to actually help build the stunt for the base and mounter.

Stand in the position where the mounter or base is most likely to fall. As the base and mounter attempt the stunt, maintain contact with the mounter at all times. Move with the stunt as it is built. Trying to steady an unstable mount or catch someone as she falls is not easy, so keep your eyes on the stunt and maintain contact until the dismount is complete. Spotters must be used until a stunt is perfected.

The following photographs show proper climbing technique. Study each photograph carefully before you attempt the stunt. Dismounts are not pictured, but follow the general rule for dismounting—reverse the climbing technique you used for the mount. Always remember the importance of spotting and seek the assistance of a qualified coach for advanced stunts.

BASE: Hold same position.
MOUNTER: Jump up; press down with hands; place body on base's lower back; hold on with legs (do not sit); point toes.

Knees on Back

BASE: Stand with feet a shoulder's width apart; knees slightly bent; hands on thighs, above knees; arms locked; back flat; head up.

MOUNTER: Stand directly behind base; one hand on lower back, other hand on shoulder for support.

BASE: Hold same position.

MOUNTER: Press down with hands; place shins on base's lower back; balance; kneel up with hips, shoulders in line; point toes.

Table-Top Stand

Start
BASE: Stand with feet shoulder width apart, knees slightly bent; hands on thighs, above knees; arms locked back flat; head up.
MOUNTER: Stand directly behind base with foot "in pocket," one hand on lower back, the other hand on shoulder for support.

Knees on Back Drop to Pony Mount

CLIMBING UP
BASE: Stand with feet shoulders' width apart; knees slightly bent; hands on thighs, above knees; arms locked; buck flat; head up.
MOUNTER: Use "step lock" technique, one foot then the other; keep head up and stand up slowly. Feet are placed in hip-lower back area.
FINISH

BASE: Hold same position. Legs straight, heels together, toes turned out.

Side Sit

BASE: Stand in right lunge position; bend knee directly over foot; right arm around mounter's waist.
MOUNTER: Stand behind base's lunged leg; left arm around base's neck, on shoulder.

BASE: Hold same position; tighten arm around mounter's waist and hold.
MOUNTER: Place left shin on base's lunged leg next to base's hip; place right shin next to left.

'Bama Sit

BASE: Stand in right lunge (knee directly over foot); right arm around mounter's waist.

MOUNTER: Stand in front of base's bent leg; pick up left knee and place shin on base's leg, next to hip; left arm around base's neck and shoulder.

BASE: Tighten arm around mounter's waist to hold; left arm catches mounter's right ankle and holds.

MOUNTER: Weight over left shin; swing up right leg (base will catch and hold); leg and back must be straight.

Side Stand

BASE: Stand in right lunge (knee directly over foot); right hand on mounter's calf.

MOUNTER: Stand behind base's lunged leg; place near foot into pocket; hands on shoulders.

BASE: Stand remains the same; support mounter's inside leg; hands above knee, pull down on leg; hold next to body.

MOUNTER: Use step lock technique; place left foot on base's upper leg, next to right foot. Press down on shoulders; place far foot next to near foot.

Rear Thigh Stand

BASE: Feet wide apart; knees bent, back straight—slight lean forward; hands on thighs, above knees; elbows locked.

MOUNTER: Stand behind base; hands on base's shoulders; place foot in pocket on bases upper leg-hip area.

BASE: Hold same position; arm position optional.

MOUNTER: Use step lock technique; place foot on base's left leg, close to hip; lean slightly forward; knees rest against base's back.

L-Stand

BASE: Stand in right lunge; right arm holds mounter's leg above knee.
MOUNTER: Stand behind base; place hands on base's shoulders; place foot in pocket on base's upper thigh, close to hip.

BASE: Hand above knee; pull down into body. As mounter steps up, catch her left leg at angle with your left hand; lock elbow.
MOUNTER: Step lock technique on right foot; lift left leg out to side (base will catch left ankle); tighten upper body. Shoulder, right hip, right knee, and right foot should form a line; arms position optional.

Stag Catch

BASE: Stand directly behind mounter; one arm around mounter's waist; other behind knee.
MOUNTER: Stand in front of base.

BASE: Hook mounter's right leg, above the knee, with bend of elbow.
MOUNTER: Jump straight up, then tip to left; extend right leg; bend left leg at knee, toe touches right knee.

Victory Mount

BASE: Lunge forward on foot (lunge low enough so mounter can step up easily); clasp hands behind back.
MOUNTER: Stand behind base; place hand on base's shoulders; place foot in base's hands.

BASE: Maintain same position.
MOUNTER: Step straight up onto right foot; support by pressing down with hands on base's shoulders; bring left knee to base's left shoulder.

BASE: Maintain same position.
MOUNTER: Use bent support leg for balance.

Straddle Shoulder Sit

BASE: Stand and lunge to right; grasp right calf from behind.
MOUNTER: Stand behind base; right foot on base's upper leg, close to right hip; both hands on base's shoulders.

BASE: Feet remain in same position; slide hand above mounter's knee and support.
MOUNTER: Step up and lock right leg; swing left leg over base's left shoulder.
Note: Base and mounter must time arms and legs together.

BASE: Once mounter has left leg over and puts weight on, grasp left leg above knee, balance, and stand up and lock both legs.
MOUNTER: Release hands as you sit on base's shoulders, tuck legs behind base, back straight, hands on hips.

Shoulder Stand

BASE: Stand in right lunge; reach out and back to take mounter's hands.

MOUNTER: Stand behind base; step up with right foot on base's upper leg, close to right hip; take base's hands.

BASE: Feet remain in same position; pull slightly forward and support as mounter presses down on hands.

MOUNTER: Step straight up on right foot; press on base's hands for support; place left foot on base's left shoulder.

BASE: After mounter has placed both feet on shoulders, straighten to full stand; let go, one hand at a time, and grasp around back of mounter's upper calves; pull gently forward with hands, and gently push head back.

MOUNTER: After placing left foot, place right foot on shoulder (keep eyes looking forward—not down); let go one hand at a time, as you stand, gently press shins against back of base's head; place hands on hips.

Star

BASE: Deep lunge position; hands on backs of legs.
MOUNTER: Stand behind base; feet apart; hands on base's shoulders.

BASE: As mounter jumps up, slide hands up back of hips; fingers points down.
MOUNTER: Jump up; straddle and extend legs (point toes) place legs on bases's upper arms; close to shoulders; lean forward slightly.

Double Stunt Sequence
(L-Stand to Straddle Shoulder Sit to Front Thigh Stand)

Base and mounter prepare
for an L-stand.

Base and mounter hit L-
stand.

BASE: Bring mounter's left leg over your left shoulder; bring feet together and come to full stand as mounter is seated; hold mounter's lower legs.
MOUNTER: Slide over onto base's right shoulder; sit as base positions your left leg; tuck feet behind base's back.

BASE: Step to side; feet wide apart; knees bent.
MOUNTER: Place feet on base's upper thighs; feet turned in pocket.

BASE: Hold mounter's legs above knees; duck head. As mounter stands, base leans back until arms are extended; keep back straight.
MOUNTER: Stand up straight; lean slightly forward; back straight—not arched.

Novelty Stunt (Reverse Bama Sit)

Lunge Heal Stretch

MOUNTER: Use step lock technique, then grab heel and stretch, inside holding hand of base.

BASE: Inside arm pulls down on thigh. Outside arm straight, holding hand of mounter.

Novelty Stunt (Liberty Thigh Stand)

BASE: Hands above knee; pull down into body; as mounter steps up catch leg in L stand position then bend knee and place foot on shoulder.

MOUNTER: Use step lock technique; raise leg for "L" stand position then remain tight and stretch tall through finish.

Double Base Torch

BASES: Both are in deep side lunge, side by side, feet overlapping, base on right; prepare to support mounter; support leg with arm behind knee.
MOUNTER: Stand behind and between both bases; place foot in pocket of left base; hands on shoulders.

Climbing in Double Base Torch

Bases remain tight; base on left, pull down and in on thigh of mounter. Mounter use step lock technique; step into pocket of base on left with hands supported on shoulders; place knee on shoulder of right base.

CHEER WITH PARTNER STUNT

Two Bits

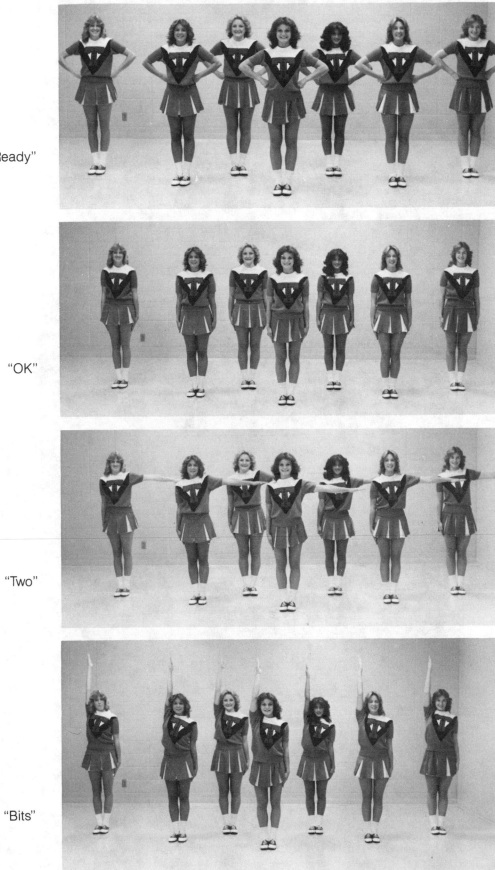

"Ready"

"OK"

"Two"

"Bits"

"Four"

"Bits"

"Six bits"

"A dollar"

"All for"

"Park Hill"

"Stand"

(pause)

"Up"

"And holler!"

Hints and Advice on Performing Partner Stunts

BASE:
- Must be firm and balanced.
- Do not watch mounter, unless necessary.
- Keep eye contact with crowd.
- Center weight and keep feet flat.
- Never walk to balance a stunt.
- Stayed poised no matter how strenuous the stunt.

MOUNTER:
- Must have control of body.
- Be aware of pointed toes; controlled, flexed legs; pulled-up mid-section; shoulders back and squared; arms placed; head up.
- When climbing or jumping onto the base, always press straight down, NEVER pull or push.
- Distribute your weight as evenly as possible.
- Always use the step lock technique.

BOTH BASE AND MOUNTER:
- Head up . . . facial confidence is important for the crowd to see and helps build mental confidence for partners.
- Spotters are a must until stunt is mastered.
- Use the signal word "DOWN" if one of you must unexpectedly dismount.
- Decide on what arm motions, dismount, etc., will be used before you try a stunt. NEVER talk during a stunt unless absolutely necessary.
- Keep eyes ahead . . . don't lose eye contact. The exception would be a head movement, as part of a cheer.
- Always perfect a stunt before performing it in public.
- Remember the importance of warm-ups and safety.
- Maintain tight body control at all times.

10
Pyramids

A pyramid is a series of double stunts involving three or more people. Pyramids are built not to "show off," but to add variety and eye-catching routines which enhance a squad's performance and its ability to establish a line of communication with the crowd.

Pyramids are usually performed during official breaks or before or after athletic events. They are generally incorporated into a cheer, a chant, or a routine choreographed to music. Sometimes the actual building of a pyramid, combined with a yell, is used as a cheer.

Bases, mounters, and spotters comprise all pyramids. The bases make up the bottom and any other level in a pyramid on which mounters are lifted or supported. The mounters form the upper level(s) of the pyramid by climbing or being placed onto the bases. Every person in a pyramid plays a vital role in the safe execution of a pyramid and should, therefore, have total confidence in her responsibilities. If one person feels shaky or insecure, the entire pyramid could collapse, resulting in injuries.

A pyramid is executed in three basic phases: 1) the building; 2) the completed pyramid; and 3) the dismount. Each phase demands timing and concentration from everyone.

The way in which a pyramid is learned is extremely important and can determine whether it will be performed correctly and safely. A pyramid should be described and taught by one person. While this person is teaching, the entire squad must be quiet and attentive. As the pyramid is described, you should picture in your mind what it will look like, where you will be positioned, and what your responsibilities will be. One way to make learning easier is to draw stick-figure diagrams or use photographs, such as those on the following pages, when describing a pyramid. By doing this, your squad will have fewer problems building the pyramid smoothly, with no injuries.

Total silence is also very important as you begin to practice building a pyramid (the words or musical counts should be added after the pyramid has been mastered). If someone should lose balance, weaken, or slip, they can indicate this by simplying saying "down" or "dismount." If everyone has remained quiet, they will hear this and can quickly come down (in reverse order only), so no one will fall or get hurt.

Since pyramids sometimes involve an entire squad, it may be necessary to find outside spotters during your practices. Make sure that all spotters know which mounter(s) they are responsible for and that they are knowledgeable and dynamic in their spotting. A good rule of thumb is one spotter for each mounter over two-people high.

In general, there are two primary methods for spotting. The first involves a mounter dismounting or falling feet first with arms extended above the head. The spotter grasps the mounter about the waist and below the buttocks with the head in front. The second technique is used when a mounter is falling in such a way that she will strike the ground other than feet first. The spotter then "cradles" the mounter, breaking her fall with the legs and arms. Both of these methods can be used by either one or two spotters for each mounter. These techniques should be practiced by all members of a squad on a regular basis. Remember, the primary goal of a spotter is to ensure a mounter's safety by keeping the head from striking the ground.

Another important learning method which can help ensure safe practice and performance of pyramids is that of building pyramids by parts from the ground up. After each member of the pyramid fully understands her job, the various double stunts which comprise a pyramid should be practiced to performance quality. These should then be added piece by piece from the ground up until the completed pyramid is finally executed. Always use plenty of spotters during this critical learning period as this is the time when most injuries occur.

Safety can be increased by the use of spotters as well as through the cooperation and mature, serious attitude of each squad member. Pyramid building is fun, but it can be dangerous if someone is clowning around or not concentrating.

If you are incorporating a pyramid into a cheer or chant, or to a musical beat, you should follow the rhythm closely. For example, the bases should get into position on a particular word, count, or beat. The mounters should follow by taking their positions on another word, count, or beat. This procedure should continue until the entire pyramid has been built. If you lose your timing or rhythm, the building of your pyramid will look clumsy and awkward.

Mounters should use the "step lock" method of climbing. The mounter must place her foot in the correct place and then lock her knee and leg in place. After locking leg, the mounter then lifts her other leg and continues climbing. Using this method will help your technique and increase your safety in practice.

Once the pyramid is up, squad members should "lock" or hold their positions for at least three counts. This will allow the crowd to see and enjoy the formation. Head motions can be used during this time to emphasize any words that are being said.

Dismounting from a pyramid is just as important as building a pyramid. The dismount should also be timed to the rhythm of the cheer, chant, or musical beat. Mounters should come down in reverse order (last person first) on specific words or counts. Once everyone is down, the cheer should continue unless the pyramid was the ending of the cheer. If it ended the cheer, it should be followed by an organized finishing motion called a "period."

Safety rules and guidelines in your state, school, or organization must be followed carefully to prevent accidents while building pyramids. Injuries will occur if rules are not followed. Be sure to check rulings in your school system and athletic associations and organizations for pyramid restrictions.

Remember when building the pyramids illustrated in this chapter that total concentration is a must. Be sure to read the helpful hints at the end of the chapter.

182

Hints and Advice on Building Pyramids

- Always have plenty of well-trained, dynamic spotters available when building pyramids.
- Build the pyramid one level at a time.
- Mount pyramid by using "step lock" method.
- Maintain the rhythm of the cheer, chant, or music while building and dismounting a pyramid.
- Plan formation by placing each person in position before you build.
- Hold the pyramid for at least three counts.
- Dismount in reverse order, last person first. Know dismount before building pyramid.
- Finish the pyramid with a "period" motion.
- All members must know their responsibilities and concentrate.
- All heads should be up. Glance down only for foot placement.
- Bases should not watch mounters as they approach; look only for placement of the foot or arm.
- Always SMILE . . . make it look easy.
- If there are arm motions, they should be sharp and timed.
- Toes should be pointed if feet are up.
- The squad should continue a cheer or yell while the pyramid is being built; the pyramid should take the crowd by surprise.
- Have fun with pyramids. Start with basic, easy pyramids and work up to the harder ones.
- Remember, the best pyramids need not be the most difficult ones. To increase safety, emphasize creativity instead of difficulty.

11

Pompon Routines

Dance routines and pompon routines are used primarily to excite and motivate your crowds during athletic events.

Cheerleaders generally perform pompon "fillers" (short pompon routines that are repeated over and over) whenever the pep band begins to play during a game. Some cheerleading squads, however, do not perform pompon routines at all, as their schools have separate drill teams, pompon squads or songleading squads that are responsible for performing routines during half-times.

Pompon routines should, ideally, be performed to live music provided by a pep band. If your school does not have a pep band that performs during games, recorded music can be substituted. If recorded music is used, your routines will almost always be performed only during halftime or official breaks.

Common Styles of Dance Routines.

There are many different types and styles of pompon routines used across the country. The most common types are listed below:

1. high kick
2. pompon (used for most routines and *all* fight songs)
3. modern jazz
4. novelty (such as the performance of the "jitterbug" to Fifties' music)

The type of routine that is performed depends upon the musical selection. It is quite effective to combine various styles, providing they complement one another. For example, high kick and pompon can be combined. The tempo of the music should dictate what type of routine is to be used.

One of the most common steps (foot motions) used in routines is called the "Bruin high step" or the "two step." This step is a quick, exciting prance that can be incorporated into almost any type of routine, particularly high kick and pompon. You can learn this step by practicing running in place. As you land on your right foot, the ball of your left foot should be lightly touching the floor. Hop quickly to your left foot and touch the ball of your right foot lightly to the floor. Repeat this until it becomes natural. Gradually increase your pace to the rhythm of: step/touch, step/touch, etc.

Keys to Performing an Exciting Routine

The keys to performing an exciting, effective pompon routine are precision and repetition.

1. Precision. Since routines are performed by groups, precision (movement performed in unison) is essential. To incorporate precision successfully into a routine, all movements must be clean and definite. Movements that cannot be broken into parts and assigned explicit counts should be avoided. Isolation movements are most important to a routine's precision. This means that when you are moving one part of your body you should de-emphasize the rest of your body. For example, if you want your audience to observe an intricate foot step, don't distract their attention with wild arm or head movements, keep your arm movements simple and insignificant. The simple rule of precision is: assign a count to every movement of the arms, feet and head.

2. Repetition. Repetition is most important in routines, as audiences rarely appreciate a movement the first time it is performed. They should see a movement more than once if you want it to have any impact. It is sometimes hard to decide upon the amount of repetition needed in a routine, but your music will help you. You can usually repeat steps when the music, itself, repeats.

Once you understand the importance of precision and repetition in your routines, you can begin to choreograph a routine. A routine, of course, consists of dance movements. If you are not familiar with dance movements you can learn them by: 1) taking dance lessons; 2) watching cheerleaders perform pompon routines; 3) creating your own movements.

Creating Dance Movements

Creating your own movements may sound hard, but is really quite simple. All you need to do is stand in front of a mirror and begin practicing the "Bruin high step." As you are doing this, add some of the basic arm motions and their variations (see Chapter 5). Explore what you can do by varying the position of your arms, legs or head. What effect can you create by looking in the opposite direction, or adding a kick or a turn? The more you experiment, the more ideas and movements you will create. Keep in mind that all of your movements should flow together smoothly.

Since your ultimate goal is to organize and create a routine, you will need to have a variety of different movements. Once your movements have been created you are ready to incorporate them into a routine.

Choreographing your movements into steps involves counting to music. If you've never taken dance lessons and do not know how to count, here is a simple method that will teach you to count in eights: Select a record with a lively tempo. Listen for the basic beat of the music and begin clapping in time to that beat. As you are clapping, start to count out loud . . . 1, 2, 3, 4, 5, 6, 7, 8, 1, 2, 3, 4 . . . and so on until the music has ended. Every count of eight represents a step.

When making up a routine you combine steps into segments. A segment usually consists of four steps (or 32 counts). By choreographing different segments and then combining them, you have created a routine. You can make up an effective segment by using either of the following methods:

Method 1: Choose a step that lasts 16 counts. Repeat that step twice to make 32 counts.
Method II: Choose two different steps, each lasting 8 counts. Then alternate step 1, step 2, step 1, step 2, to make 32 counts.

By using these methods when creating segments, you will be assured of having the necessary repetition in your routine.

Remember as you are choreographing to begin your routine with an eye-catching introduction and finish with an exact, exciting ending. The exception to this is if you are making up pompon "fillers." Since fillers are merely sets of steps that are designed to be repeated over and over, an introduction and ending are not necessary. The steps in a filler should either be in 8 or 16 counts so they can be adapted easily to any music.

How To Practice a Routine.

Since most schools do not require cheerleader candidates to perform pompon routines during tryouts, you probably won't have to worry about routines until you are on a squad. If you want, however, to get a head start on everyone else by knowing a pompon routine before being elected, you should begin practicing now.

As with every other aspect of physical cheerleading, practicing pompon routines must begin with proper warming-up exercises. The basic exercises shown in Chapter III should be done, as well as leg exercises, such as kicks and splits.

It is important that you learn every step correctly as you are practicing. To accomplish this, you should practice using the segment method. Start with the first four or five steps. Once you have learned these steps, practice the next four or five steps, adding them to those you have already learned. Continue this procedure until you have learned the entire routine.

You must be sure to count as you are practicing, and watch yourself in a mirror to make sure your motions are perfectly placed and executed. Have someone watch you perform your routine once you have learned it so they can offer constructive criticism.

Once you become a cheerleader and practice pompon routines as a squad, unity will be one area you will have to work very hard on. It takes many hours to perfect a routine so that every member of a squad is performing the same steps in unison.

Remember as you are practicing to smile and have a pleasant facial expression. Hold your head high to instill a look of confidence. Work on the form of any kicks that might be used in the routine (point your toes and keep your legs very straight). Practice with personality and excitement. You need to develop a great deal of presence and poise. It's up to you to make your audience feel comfortable no matter what the performing conditions. Your audience should only see you looking poised, confident, and happy. Your energy should penetrate the audience so they feel uplifted by watching you.

KICKS

Kick Levels

Knee Kicks

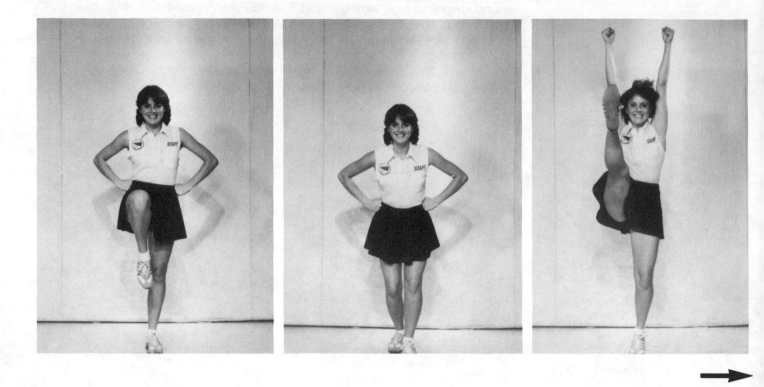

Turned-Out Knee Kicks

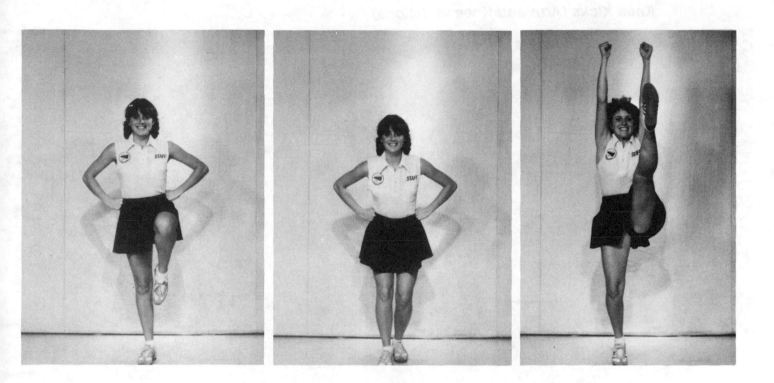

Knee Kicks (Arm and Knee Variations)

Herkie Kicks

Herkie Kick Variation

Pretzel Kicks

Side Kicks

POMPON ROUTINE FILLERS

Dance Routine—40 Counts Dance Routine A

(Counts 1, 2, 3, 4)
Arms at side; legs to-
gether.

(Count 5)
Bruin with right foot;
Arms circle around;
clap.

(Count 6)
Bruin with left foot;
clap.

(Count 2)
Cross right leg over left.

(Count 3)
Turn to back; arms
down to side.

(Count 4)
Left lunge; right arm out in
buckets;
left arm to shoulder.

(Count 7)
Bruin with right foot.

(Count 8)
Bruin with left foot.

(Count 1)
Arms in "T";
Back hop kick with right
leg.

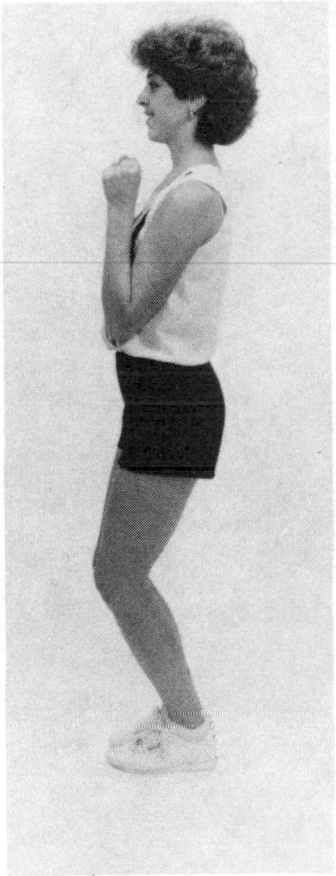

(Count 5)
Arms into shoulders.

(Count 6)
Right arm straight;
left arm bent;
right leg straight side kick.

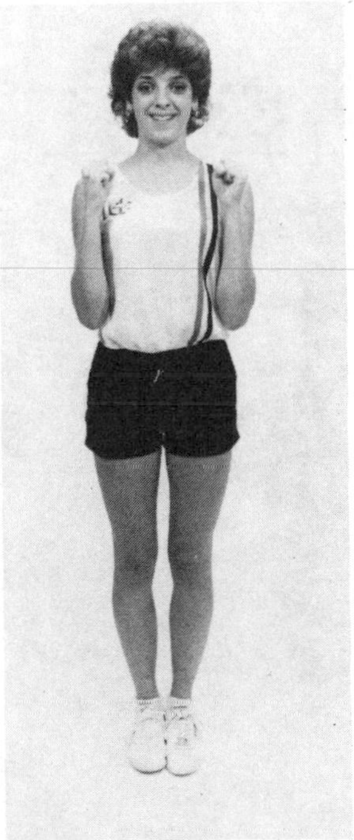

(Count 7, 8)
Arms in daggers.

(Count 1)
Right leg out;
hands clasp down in front.

(Count 2)
Left leg out;
arms clasp; bent elbows
up.

(Count 3)
Right leg out;
Arms in high "V".

(Count 7, 8, 1, 2)
Left arm circle;
right arm comes straight
down;
legs straighten.

(Count 3, 4)
Bend at waist;
arms wrapped around
waist.

(Count 5, 6)
Left lunge;
right arm in high "V";
Left arm down to side.

(Count 4)
Left leg out;
arms bent "V".

(Count 5)
Left lunge;
right arm diagonal;
left arm straight up.

(Count 6)
Legs stay in left lunge;
right arm out;
left arm bent.

(Count 7)
Straighten legs;
arms bent in daggers.

(Count 8, 1, 2)
Bend at waist;
arms straight back.

(Count 3)
Right arm straight out;
left arm down to side;
right cuban.

(Count "and")
Arms in daggers;
legs straighten.

(Count 4, 5, 6)
Left arm straight up;
right arm straight down;
left cuban.

(Count 7)
Arms in "T";
legs straight;
head turned.

(Count 8)
Arms in high "V";
left leg out, bent in front

Bruin High Step
(With Basic Arm Motions and Turns—32 Counts)

(Counts 1–8.) Feet together; hands at waist.

(Count 1.) Weight on right foot, touch left; arms—daggers.

(Count 2.) Weight on left foot, touch right; arms—vertical up.

(Count 6.) Weight on left foot, touch right; right arm—vertical up, left arm—dagger.

(Count 7.) Weight on right foot, touch left; left arm—vertical up, right arm—dagger.

(Count 8.) Weight on left foot, touch right; arms horizontal, right arm bent at elbow, fist at shoulder.

(Count 3.) Weight on right foot, touch left; arms horizontal.

(Count 4.) Weight on left foot, touch right; arms scoop back and down, passing waist; hands stop together in front at waist level (elbows bent at waist).

(Count 5.) Weight on right foot, touch left; arms horizontal, left arm bent at elbow, fist at shoulder.

(Count 1.) Step sideways right foot; right arm horizontal, left hand on hip.

(Count 2.) With left foot, step across the front of right leg; pivot to back; arms same.

(Count 3.) With right foot, step across and behind left leg; return to front; arms same.

(Count 4.) Weight on right foot, touch left; left hand remains on hip, right arm scoops behind and through; hand stops at waist.

(Count 5.) Step sideways with left foot; right hand on hip, left arm horizontal.

(Count 6.) With right foot, step across the front of left, pivot to back; arms same.

(Count 2.) Weight on left foot, touch right; arms open to left diagonal (left arm up).

(Count 3.) Weight on right foot, touch left; arms in right diagonal, bent at elbows.

(Count 4.) Weight on left foot, touch right; arms open to right diagonal (right arm up).

(Count 5.) Feet together, knees bent; arms—vertical down.

(Count 7.) With left foot, step across and behind right leg, return to front; arms same.

(Count 8.) Weight on left foot, touch right; right hand remains on hip; left arm scoops behind and through; hand stops at waist.

(Count 1.) Weight on right foot, touch left; arms in left diagonal, bent at elbows.

(Count 6.) Jump straight up, feet together; arms horizontal.

(Count 7.) Land on balls of feet; knees bent.

(Count 8.) Begin over.

Dance Routine B

(Count 1, 2, 3, 4, 5)
Bend at waist;
arms down;
head down.

(Count 6)
Start straightening up;
keep head down.

(Count 7)
Continue straightening up.

(Count 3)
Knees bent;
left arm bent to right side;
right arm down to side;
head to the right side.

(Count 4)
Left arm straight out;
head to the left;
right arm down to side;
bent knees.

(Count 5)
Right arm bent;
head to left;
knees bent.

(Count 8)
Knees bent;
hands on back of thighs.

(Count 1)
Head to the left;
right arm bent at elbow to
the left side;
bend knees.

(Count 2)
Bend knees;
right arm straight out;
head to the right;
left arm down to side.

(Count 6)
Bend knees;
right arm to side;
left arm down to side;
head to right.

(Count 7, 8)
Bend at waist to right side;
head down;
arms on knee.

(Count 1)
Lunge to left;
left arm out to side;
right arm on hip.

(Count 2, 3, 4)
Right lunge;
right arm up;
left arm behind back.

(Count 5, 6)
Right cuban;
right arm up, bent at elbow;
left arm behind back.

(Count 3)
Switch legs;
facing back.

(Count 4)
Switch legs;
facing back.

(Count 5)
Left leg bent in front;
arms bent at elbows.

(Count 7, 8)
Face left side;
left arm straight up;
right arm on hip.

(Count 1)
Arms in "T";
right leg out in front.

(Count 2)
Turn to back;
arms down to side.

(Count 6)
Switch legs;
keep arms bent.

(Count 7)
Switch legs;
keep arms bent.

(Count 7)
Legs together;
arms bent at elbows.

(Count 8, 1)
Legs together;
head down;
hands come in on stomach.

(Count 2, 3, 4)
Right knee on floor;
left knee bent;
arms in high "V";
head back.

(Count 5, 6)
Bend at waist;
head down;
arms down.

(Count 7)
Straighten up;
arms down to side.

(Count 8)
Arms behind head;
turn to right side;
bend left knee

Fight Song C

(Count 1)
Face forward;
left leg bent up;
arms on waist.

(Count 2)
Arms on waist;
left leg back.

(Count 3)
Arms straight up;
kick with left leg.

(Count 7)
Right arm straight above head;
left arm on waist;
right knee out and bent.

(Count 8)
Turn to left side;
knees bent;
arms bent in daggers.

(Count 1)
Arms in "T";
kick with left leg.

(Count 4)
Right leg bent;
arms on waist.

(Count 5)
Right leg back;
hands on waist.

(Count 6)
Kick with right leg;
arms straight above head.

(Count 2)
Turn to right side;
arms in daggers.

(Count 3)
Kick with right leg;
arms in "T".

(Count 4)
Right leg back;
arms bent into right shoulder.

(Count 5)
Turn to right side;
knees bent;
arms bent in daggers.

(Count 6)
Kick with right leg;
arms straight out.

(Count 7)
Turn to left side;
bend knees;
arms in daggers.

(Count 2)
Left leg out in front;
arms straight above head.

(Count 3)
Arms out in "V";
left leg bent.

(Count 4)
Right arm straight above
head;
left arm down to side;
right leg back.

(Count 8)
Kick with left leg;
arms straight out.

(Count 8)
Face front;
arms in at waist.

(Count 1)
Bend knees;
bring arms up in daggers.

(Count 5)
Arms in low "V";
right leg out.

(Count 6)
Left arm straight up;
right arm straight out to
side;
right leg up.

(Count 7, hold 8)
Arms in high "V";
right leg out.

Hints and Advice on Performing Pompon Routines

- Do not count out loud or form the count number with your lips.
- When doing head motions, they should be precise.
- Point toes on all foot motions.
- Do not hunch shoulders up.
- Keep head and shoulders in line with rest of body when kicking.
- Stand tall; be proud.
- When dancing, think ahead to the next step so you can move into it smoothly.
- Keep your head up and look at the audience (it shows confidence).
- Always smile and project personality.

12

Safety

Cheerleading has always been a physical activity, but only in the last few years has it become a SERIOUS ATHLETIC ACTIVITY similar to other sports. Across America, cheerleaders have begun using their true athletic ability, and, in doing so, the skill and difficulty level of stunts, gymnastics, jumps, and pyramids has increased accordingly.

Why the Increase in Difficulty? Cheerleaders are athletically inclined and yet, with the many responsibilities of cheering, there isn't time to participate in other sports. Cheering is their sport! And as in all athletics, it is a natural desire to attempt advanced skills once you master the level you are working on. Thus, cheerleaders continually improve and increase their skill level.

Cheerleading is often a thankless task. And though you spend your time supporting everyone else, that doesn't stop you from wanting to achieve physically and to receive recognition for your efforts.

The "good old school spirit" enjoyed back in the fifties somehow went by the wayside after that golden era. Cheerleading remained basically the same through the early seventies; however school spirit began to wane. In the mid-seventies, the physical side of cheering began changing. Cheerleaders found they received a better crowd response when they increased the "entertainment" aspect of cheering. This included increasing the difficulty level of jumps, gymnastics, double stunts, dances, and especially pyramids.

Is There a Problem with Difficult Cheering Skills? The answer is yes. A lot of confusion exists regarding safety, and there exists no central administrative group that is responsible for, and understands, cheerleading enough to regulate what can and cannot be done.

Another problem exists. Cheerleading may not be a sport in itself, but it is an extremely physical activity that needs qualified coaches. In some areas cheerleading coaches are nonexistent. Every squad always has a sponsor who monitors activities; however, these people often do NOT consider themselves COACHES.

What is the Coach's Role? He or she trains and instructs the athletes. Conversely, what role does a cheerleading sponsor have? Is she or he a coach? If not, who is? Who fairly determines what cheering activities are and are not safe? Should you decide yourself what level of difficulty to attempt? Have you studied the sport enough to know what is safe? Clearly, confusion does exist.

Some state athletic associations have strict policies governing cheerleading safety; others claim cheerleading is not within their jurisdiction because it is not a sport. Some school boards or school principals set up recommendations or guidelines. Quite often, however, no rules exist until an injury occurs. When this happens, various administrative groups scramble to set rules in the crisis period following an injury, even though their rules may be questionable and based on little factual data.

What Can Be Done to Keep Injuries From Escalating? Though some might wish it so, going back to the fifties style of cheerleading just won't work in our schools today. High-level skills will remain in cheerleading to some degree. Cheerleaders and cheerleading coaches (sponsors) must educate themselves in every way possible to learn proper techniques and methods to reduce injury risk.

If you don't make the effort to learn and establish rules, don't be upset when someone with little cheering knowledge does it for you. Their rules may not be fair, but they are better than none at all! Learn and practice the following rules:

1. ESTABLISH STRICT PRACTICE AND PERFORMANCE RULES. Ignoring safety rules or "pleading ignorance" is dangerous for cheerleaders, sponsors, and schools. Make it a strict squad rule that you always exercise extreme caution when learning, practicing, and performing your physical skills.
2. BE ESPECIALLY CAUTIOUS WITH PYRAMIDS. Several squad members are required to actually climb on each other, which leaves room for many errors.
3. CONDITION THOROUGHLY to prevent sprained ankles, muscle pulls, shin splints, and other injuries common to aerobic activities.
4. USE SPOTTERS. As you learn to perform stunts, pyramids, and gymastics, always use spotters who understand exactly what you are attempting to do.
5. ATTEND A SUMMER WORKSHOP TO LEARN FROM PROFESSIONALS. The International Cheerleading Foundation conducts nearly 200 annual summer camps across the nation to teach cheerleaders and their sponsors proper technique and injury prevention.* These professional cheerleading instructors study the activity year round and have been doing so for over twenty years. Attending camp is vital to learning the latest skill technique and methods of injury prevention.

The following chart will give you a beginning set of guidelines to increase safety on your squad.

How to Reduce Injury Risk

KNOWLEDGE OF SKILL
- Proper instruction should be received before any skill is attempted.

*Write for a free brochure on safe cheerleading and a listing of summer workshops for cheerleaders c/o ICF, Box 7088, Shawnee Mission, Kansas 66207.

- Proper instruction includes a "beginning to end" progression of the skill.
- A cheerleader should never be required to do more than her ability level.
- Proper technique and spotting must be a priority.

SPOTTING
- Use spotters when learning all gymnastics, double stunts, and pyramids. In pyramids, use one spotter for each person that is a mounter.
- Spotters must learn the correct position for the spotter in each skill.

ATTITUDE
- Each cheerleader must understand the "sport" of cheerleading and be willing to work hard on technique and safety.
- The squad must have a serious attitude about performing skills.
- Everyone must concentrate during practices and performances.
- No skills should ever be attempted when a squad member does not feel like doing so.
- An attitude of teamwork needs to drive the squad to higher goals; however, you must also be able to recognize your limits.

FACILITIES
- Practice and performing areas must be safe.
- Avoid cheering on cement or similar hard surfaces.
- Use gymnastic mats whenever possible.
- Make sure lighting (visibility) is good.

WEATHER
- Avoid performing difficult skills when the weather is extremely hot, cold, wet, or windy.

USE OF STUNTS, PYRAMIDS, AND GYMNASTICS
- Never perform difficult routines near the end of a game or practice when the squad is extremely fatigued.
- Make sure you have ample time to perform stunts, pyramids, or gymnastics.
- Only perform stunts you have completely mastered.

CONDITIONING
- Initiate a well-planned program utilizing flexibility, strength, and endurance exercises.
- Always include this program in your squad practices as well as before games.
- Increase your aerobic endurance so you will be able to cheer energetically and safely throughout an entire game.
- Stress good eating habits, nutrition, and weight control for maximum athletic efficiency.

13

Leadership

From the very first moment you become a cheerleader, you will find that your responsibilities go far beyond improving your jumps and gymnastics and learning to perform with your squad. Your most important job as a cheerleader is to influence and direct people. In other words, BE A LEADER, in front of a crowd, at school, in your community . . . at all times.

School and Community Leadership

Every group needs a leader. A football team needs a captain and a coach. Organizations and clubs need presidents. Armies and navies need generals and admirals. And in the hands of these leaders falls the job of organizing people, outlining a plan for action with the people, and motivating them to help carry out the plan.

CHEERLEADING WILL TEACH YOU MANY CHARACTER-BUILDING TRAITS—teamwork, money management, concern for others, speaking to a crowd, goal setting, public relations, and the list goes on and on. More important and valuable than anything else, CHEERLEADING TEACHES LEADERSHIP. Today, cheerleaders are school leaders; tomorrow they are leaders within families, communities, churches, and our government! Now that's exciting!

Did you know that many schools across the United States have powerful school spirit programs due to the leadership of their cheerleaders? School PRIDE is high; enthusiasm and support for the school is strong; and an enjoyable, concerned attitude for everyone involved with the school prevails. What is the trick? How can you get started doing the same thing at your school?

ESTABLISH YOUR REPUTATION. From the moment you become a cheerleader, you will be in the spotlight—EVERYWHERE! Your face will be recognized at school and in your community. Your teachers will notice you more, as will your principal. Your picture will be in the newspaper. People will see you in front of the crowd. You will be recognized in the town at fund raisers and community service projects. Students will watch you, follow you, copy what you do and say—even talk about you and possibly be jealous of you. You have stepped into a leadership position and now you must prove you are worthy of the position.

Guidelines for establishing your reputation as a school leader.

- Be a leader in your classrooms. Work hard on your grades (they always come first!).
- Be kind and considerate to everyone.
- Demonstrate that you set goals, you are organized, and you accomplish what you set out to.
- Make sure your appearance is everything it can be. Set an example.
- Be prompt and dependable at all times.
- Go out of your way to help out when you see someone in need whether you know that person or not!
- Learn names and use them.
- Be respectful to everyone.
- Get involved.
- Keep your conduct above reproach at all times.

ESTABLISH YOUR SQUAD'S REPUTATION Teamwork is necessary to change the attitude at your school. Every cheerleader on your squad needs to work toward developing good school and community relations.

Your squad rules, philosophy, and goals should be established first, so you will each be working toward the same goal. Keep in mind the following guidelines:

- Discuss and determine the needs of your school.
- Set your goals for the year beginning with the effect you want to have on the school and community. (Also, know your physical cheering skill goals—and how you plan to become an impressive performing team.)
- Follow the rules outlined in your cheerleader constitution at all times.
- Work your plan of action!

SCHOOL RELATIONS. In order to improve or change the attitudes of others concerning cheerleading, your squad must be seen as a caring, supportive squad. Take the first step in showing thoughtfulness and appreciation toward others. Do not be disappointed if you don't see immediate results. Establishing genuine friendships and trust takes time.

There are hundreds of ways to improve your squad's relationship within the school. Recognize club activities and support them. You can also recognize individual student accomplishments. Be a friend to everyone. A smile goes a long way from someone who is in the limelight to someone who is not! Support your school band, drill team, and pep club. Show them you are not a rival school group. Why not welcome new students to your school? Get them started on the right foot by getting acquainted and making them feel at home.

How do you establish good working relationships with your teachers and school administrators? Try remembering them on birthdays and holidays. A small gift for the janitors or the cafeteria workers will always be treasured. Why not do the same for your principal? Place refreshments in the teachers' lounge or offer to be teachers' aides at the beginning or end of school. Use your imagination but do take time to pay attention and respect to these people.

COMMUNITY RELATIONS. Since the cheerleader's reputation stretches far beyond the boundaries of the school, it is important to be identified as an important part of the community. Get involved in community activities and service projects. How rewarding it is to give to others! The more the public can see you in a positive, community-involved activity, the more supportive they will be of your spirit-raising program. Try any of the following ideas:

1. *Sponsor Clean-up Days*—Contact the city council to get permission to clean up a specific area. Why not turn the lot that has been an "eye sore" in your area into a playground or park. This would be an excellent father-daughter activity.
2. *Plan Senior Citizen Activities*—This group can never get too much attention. Check with the local nursing home for permission to hold special activities and visits. Look around your community for lonely senior citizens to help. Some activities that could be planned are as follows:
A. *Adopt a grandparent*—Establish a relationship with a senior citizen who has few visitors. Visit regularly, sharing experiences and remembering all special occasions.
B. *Have a songfest*—Most senior citizens love to listen to and participate in singing. Share your talents with them. Learn some ol' time songs from their era to share with them.
C. *Visit a nursing home*—Each week have several cheerleaders drop in and visit with patients. The cheerleaders could assist in letter writing for the patients or just sit and chat.
D. *Treat to a ballgame*—Arrange for chearleader parents to take several elderly people who still love to watch ballgames to be the cheerleaders' special guests at a game.
3. *Assist Charities in Raising Money*—A friendly, pretty cheerleader in uniform is a tremendous boost to any fund-raising drive. The cheerleaders will be the big winners when they help others less fortunate than themselves. The sense of self-worth and personal satisfaction received from helping others is well worth the time and energy involved.

   Some of the successful ways cheerleaders can raise money for charities are: run or walk-a-thons, road blocks, door-to-door solicitations, flea markets or garage sales, talent/cheering performances, and dunking booths.

   Cheerleaders across the nation are noted for helping the needy. Traditionally cheerleaders sponsor food drives, toys for tots at Christmas, food baskets at Thanksgiving, and sending needy children to day camps. Cheerleaders find it rewarding to participate in organizations such as "A Child's Wish Come True," which grants a wish to a terminally ill child, and youth ranches for homeless teenagers.
4. *Participate in various community activities* such as:
   Special Olympics
   Pep rallies for classes of mentally retarded students
   Cheer show for a grammar school

Talent program for civic club meetings
Sign making for community events
Hostess for community events
Camp counselors for camps for handicapped children
Grand openings for new stores
Visits to the children's wing at a hospital
Visits to a Veteran's hospital
Performance at grade-school athletic banquets

Crowd Leadership

The image of a cheerleader being silly, popular, pretty, and, for the most part, ineffective in leading a crowd is a thing of the past. At times you may have to battle this old reputation; however, as cheerleaders have become more effective, people have become appreciative of the purpose and work involved in cheerleading.

Leadership and crowd control at an athletic event is a cheerleader's responsibility. You need to become an expert in raising enthusiasm, generating spirit, and controlling a restless crowd. That is no easy task, considering your crowd includes students, teachers, parents, children, and community members!

You need to gain a crowd's respect, as any leader must, before you can ask them to support you. If you want your crowd to follow your cheers and chants, first establish your cheering expertise and your talents as a school leader. If your squad appears unorganized, self-centered, and unknowledgeable about the game, what fan in their right mind would follow you? (They might laugh at you but they won't follow you!)

What type of behavior will impress your fans? Talented, unified, mature cheerleaders who pay attention to the crowd and the game instead of themselves ATTRACT the attention of an audience! Make sure your appearance is sharp, follow the leadership of your captain, and do not talk during the game. Remember you are in the spotlight at all times so act like a leader.

Your next job is to develop a rapport with your fans. Begin by focusing on your crowd. Fans glance at cheerleaders during a game, but it is your responsibility to initiate and encourage interaction with the fans. In order to instill enthusiasm and spirit in a crowd, your spirit must be genuine. You must love it, enjoy it . . . and convey this warm, enthusiastic feeling to your crowd. Just like a smile, spirit is contagious. When you have it and project it, your crowd will want to follow suit.

Cheerleaders often blame a lack of spirit on the crowd when it is not the crowd's fault. Get to know your fans and the way they behave. What makes them excited? How can you help them have fun at the games win or lose? Are your cheers and chants simple and easy to follow? Would a grown man or one of the guys in your school want to cheer with you? Think about what pleases your crowd—not just your squad. If you were in the crowd, what kinds of chants would you enjoy? Use cheers with fun rhythms and positive, colorful wording. Even if your teams have trouble winning, your fans will want to cheer with you if they are having FUN!

Many school sports crowds are poorly behaved. Fans get unruly. They yell negative things at the players, the officials, and the cheerleaders. Cheerleaders must take immediate and decisive action to not only stop bad crowd behavior, but turn it around so it is once again good and strong. Never be sarcastic or negative in cheering. If you face an unhappy crowd that insists on booing the other team or the referee, start one of your crowd's favorite chants or signal your pep band to play—anything to divert the attention of your crowd.

Remember these tips on CROWD CONTROL:

- Learn how to be an effective public speaker.
- Understand the sport you are cheering for.
- Know your crowd and work with them, not against them.
- Be creative and interesting crowd leaders.
- Develop your cheering skills.
- Be sincere and enthusiastic.
- Promote good sportsmanship.
- Act like the leader that you are!

Every time you are in the public view, you are on display, much like an actress or a politician. Your actions and words are a reflection not only of yourself, but of your entire school! A cheerleader who is respected as a good citizen and student leader is also a cheerleader who will receive the support of the crowds during the games. School leaders and crowd leadership—doing well in one will lead to success in the other!

14

Understanding Sports—
Football, Basketball, Wrestling

It goes without saying that a cheerleader should have an extensive knowledge of game rules. To know what cheer or chant is appropriate during a game, you must be aware of the game's progress at all times. You never want to catch yourself yelling "block-that-kick" when it is your team attempting the extra point after a touchdown! Nor do you want to put yourself in the awkward position of cheering at the wrong time.

Listed below are guidelines to help you know when it is appropriate to cheer and when it is not. Do remember that the attention of your crowd should be on the play, not you, when the game is in progress.

When You Should Cheer:
1. At the beginning of the game as your team runs onto the court or field
2. To encourage your team as they attempt to score
3. Following an excellent play by your team or one of your players
4. When your team has scored
5. As a player substitution on your team is being made
6. To encourage your team in their efforts to defend your goal
7. Between plays in football as well as during time-outs in football or basketball
8. To encourage and acknowledge the efforts of an injured player as he leaves the court or field
9. When the game has ended

When You Should Not Cheer:
1. As starting lineups and announcements are made over the loudspeaker
2. When a free throw is being attempted in basketball
3. If an opponent errs or is penalized
4. If a player from either team is injured
5. When the other team's cheerleaders have started a cheer
6. When the band is playing
7. When cheering would drown out the signals of either team in their huddle
8. When the quarterback is calling signals to put the ball in play

Since there are thousands of different cheers and chants, it is important that you learn what type of yell to use in different game situations. If you have an inadequate understanding of the sports you cheer for, you are more than likely leading inappropriate cheers. To test your knowledge of sports and game rules, we have prepared brief football, basketball and wrestling quizzes. If you find that you do not know many of the answers, you should meet with a coach or captain of each sport and have him/her explain the rules of the game. If this is not possible, there are books available that contain sports rules and their definitions.

FOOTBALL QUIZ
1. How long is your football field?
2. How many defensive players should be on the field?
3. How many points are scored for each of the following:
   _____ Touchdown
   _____ Field goal
   _____ Safety
   _____ Points after touchdown
4. How long is each quarter?
5. How many time-outs are given each team per half?
6. What constitutes a first down?
7. When does your team change goals?
8. How long is half-time?
9. When does a team punt?
10. How many attempts does your team have to achieve a first down?
11. Label the offensive players' positions on the following diagram:

```
     X   X   X   X   X   X   X
       X           X           X
                   X
```

12. List three common penalties.

BASKETBALL QUIZ:
1. What is the opening play of the game?
2. How many minutes are in a game?
3. How many periods are in a period?
4. How many fouls can a player have before he is removed from the game?
5. How many time-outs are allowed each team per game?
6. How many points are scored for the following:
   _____ Field goal
   _____ Free throw
7. How many players from your team should be on the court at one time?
8. Who can commit a technical foul?
9. Define the following:
   Double dribble
   Traveling
   Blocking

10. Name the player positions on your team.
11. List three common violations.
12. When a player makes a throw-in, how many seconds does he have?

WRESTLING QUIZ:

1. Describe the starting positions.
2. How many periods are possible in each match?
3. How long is each period?
4. Define the following:
   Default
   Reversal
   Takedown
5. How many points are scored for each of the following:
   ____ Takedown
   ____ Escape
   ____ Reversal
   ____ Near-fall
   ____ Time advantage
6. List two common penalties.
7. List the weight classes.

In addition to your knowledge of sports and game rules you should also be familiar with official game signals. Shown on the following pages are official football and basketball signals.

Official Football Signals*

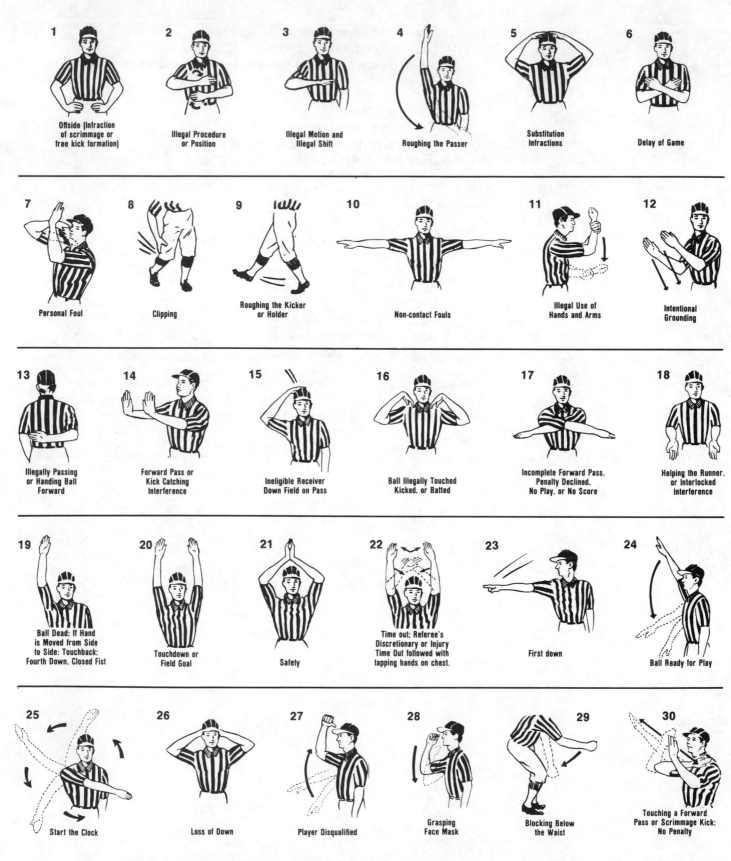

1 **Offside (Infraction of scrimmage or free kick formation)**

2 **Illegal Procedure or Position**

3 **Illegal Motion and Illegal Shift**

4 **Roughing the Passer**

5 **Substitution Infractions**

6 **Delay of Game**

7 **Personal Foul**

8 **Clipping**

9 **Roughing the Kicker or Holder**

10 **Non-contact Fouls**

11 **Illegal Use of Hands and Arms**

12 **Intentional Grounding**

13 **Illegally Passing or Handing Ball Forward**

14 **Forward Pass or Kick Catching Interference**

15 **Ineligible Receiver Down Field on Pass**

16 **Ball Illegally Touched Kicked, or Batted**

17 **Incomplete Forward Pass, Penalty Declined, No Play, or No Score**

18 **Helping the Runner, or Interlocked Interference**

19 **Ball Dead; If Hand is Moved from Side to Side: Touchback; Fourth Down. Closed Fist**

20 **Touchdown or Field Goal**

21 **Safety**

22 **Time out; Referee's Discretionary or Injury Time Out followed with tapping hands on chest.**

23 **First down**

24 **Ball Ready for Play**

25 **Start the Clock**

26 **Loss of Down**

27 **Player Disqualified**

28 **Grasping Face Mask**

29 **Blocking Below the Waist**

30 **Touching a Forward Pass or Scrimmage Kick; No Penalty**

NOTE: All personal foul signals should be preceded by Signal 7.

* Courtesy of the National Collegiate Athletic Association Publication Department.

Official Basketball Signals*

For free throw violation:
Use Signals 2 and 18

For basket interference:
Use Signals 16 or 14 and 6

* Courtesy of the National Collegiate Athletic
Association Publication Department.

15

Uniforms and Supplies

In spite of the rapid change in clothing styles over the past fifty years, the apparel of cheerleaders has not changed drastically. Skirt lengths, of course, have risen and fallen with fashion trends, but the standard cheerleader skirt and sweater and the newer skirt and vest are generally seen.

Uniforms are, naturally, designed to give a squad a unified appearance. It is important, therefore, that they be flattering as well as functional and practical.

Since your appearance is so very important, and there are so many different types and styles of uniforms on the market, you must be careful in your selection. Factors such as price, type of fabric, durability, practicality and color must be considered. It would probably be wise for your entire squad to sit down together and come up with a checklist of things you want to know about each uniform before you make your final choice.

Type of Fabric. This should be one of your first considerations. You must keep in mind the weather conditions in your area. If you cheer in cold weather during football season, you will probably want a heavier fabric, such as wool, with a matching long-sleeved sweater. If you live in a warmer climate, you might consider a sleeveless vest, a polyester jumper, or lightweight fabric for football season.

Since there is a great deal of movement involved in cheerleading, the quality of the fabric must also be determined. You don't want to have to worry about sleeves ripping out or seams popping. You need a durable, sturdy fabric that can withstand many washings or dry cleanings and will not spot badly if subjected to rain, mud, perspiration, etc. Remember, your uniform will get a lot of wear and tear, so select your fabric carefully.

Style. The style of your uniform will depend on the preferences of your squad. You should try to select a style, however, that will compliment everyone's figure. Remember that vertical stripes make tall girls look taller and horizontal stripes make heavier girls seem heavier. Length of skirts must also be checked. Be sure to select an attractive length for the entire squad.

Price. This will depend on how much each individual cheerleader can afford to spend for a uniform. You should remember that an expensive price tag does not necessarily mean you are getting the best product on the market. There are many attractive outfits that are available at reasonable prices. Some uniforms can even be handmade or you can purchase precut pieces and sew them together, yourself. Check the list of cheerleader supply houses at the end of this chapter. Write away for their catalogs and take time to compare prices and quality.

Care. Constant upkeep of your uniforms, once you have them, is important. They will continue to look fresh and will wear well if you take care of them properly. Always brush your uniform with a soft, clean brush and hang it up between wearings. If you should have to press out wrinkles, be sure to turn your uniform inside out to do so. Collars and cuffs should be pressed by placing a clean cloth over the area before ironing. If your uniform is not machine washable and begins to show soil on the neckline or cuffs, you should sponge the area lightly with a good cleaning fluid. Proper care and maintenance of your uniform will keep it looking "good as new."

Shoes. The cheerleading shoe is probably the most important part of the cheerleading uniform. Special cheerleading shoes have been developed to give the support needed for cheerleading activities. Give special attention to the sole of the cheerleading shoe to be sure it is suitable for climbing and jumping. The shoes should be comfortable, lightweight, and waterproof. The tennis shoe is the most popular shoe worn by cheerleaders; however, many squads still use the saddle oxford.

There is a wide range of color-coordinated styles of cheering shoes. Remember, it is important to wear a good shoe when practicing as well as when cheering. Tennis socks, footies, or knee socks may be worn with any shoe style you select.

Write to the International Cheerleading Foundation to receive a complete, color brochure on shoes made especially for cheerleading (Box 7088, Shawnee Mission, Kansas 66207).

Jewelry. Since the type of jewelry that can be worn by cheerleaders is limited, the following guidelines should be followed: 1) wear only small post earrings, as hoops or dangling earrings can get caught in your hair or sweater; 2) wear only short chain necklaces, long chains, especially those with trinkets on them, can fly into your face or mouth, and have been known to chip teeth; 3) bracelets and watches should fit closely to your wrist. Ideally, they should not be worn at all, but if you must, do not wear chains that can snag a sweater or dangle and become a nuisance; 4) rings should not be worn. If you are wearing a ring while clapping, you can easily injure or bruise your hand. 5) Nail polish, while not an item of jewelry, is decorative and should not be worn by cheerleaders unless the shade is skin color or clear.

Accessories. There have been some innovations in accessories during the past years. Chief among them is the all-vinyl plastic pompon which was introduced by the International Cheerleading Foundation in 1968. This pompon has now nearly replaced the delicate paper pompon.

Another key accessory is the megaphone. Painted in fancy color trim, they can add beautifully to the image you want to maintain in front of your crowds. The megaphone amplifies your voice and should be used consistently. Few, if any, megaphones can be purchased with your school colors already applied. This you must do yourself after purchasing a "blank" megaphone. They are manufactured in fiberboard, Fiberglas and plastic, and are available from most cheerleader supply companies.

Color rain ponchos and jackets made of vinyl are available. Satin-type cheerleader jackets in school colors are another popular cheerleader accessory. Night shirts, T shirts, two-toned gloves, tams, scarves, letters emblems, mascot emblems, and cheerleader jewelry are also popular items. These may be purchased at sporting-good stores or through any of the major cheerleader supply companies.

Check with the following uniform and supply companies for all your cheerleading needs:

Rally Pep and Spirit Supply
Box 7088, Shawnee Mission, Kansas 66207
(cheerleading shoes, T shirts, and jewelry)

CHEERZ! Uniforms and Sportswear
413 Broad St., Gadsden, Alabama
(uniforms and accessories)

Cheerleader Supply Company
9150 Markville Drive
Dallas, Texas 75243
(uniforms and all accessories)

Cranbarry, Inc.
2 Lincoln Ave.
P.O. Box 488
Marblehead, Massachusetts 01945
(uniforms)

Varsity Spirit Fashions
4835 Viscount Suite #1
Memphis, Tennessee 38118
(uniforms and accessories)

16
Fund Raising

Raising money for uniforms, summer camp, decorations and props for spirit activities and transportation to away games is one of the most time-consuming duties of being a cheerleader. If your school can not help you financially (ideally they should—you are, after all, an important part of the athletic program), you will continually be involved in fund-raising projects.

As with any cheerleading activity, the key to the success of your fund-raising drive is organization. Following is an easy checklist that will help you each time you prepare for a fund-raising project:

1. **Plan Your Budget.** Determine how much money you will need throughout the year.
2. **Find out restrictions.** Check with school authorities to see if any limits or restrictions have been placed on fund-raising projects. Check if restrictions apply to summer months.
3. **Decide on your fund-raising projects.** Plan carefully for a successful, fun event.
4. **Set your dates.** Keep in mind the availability of facilities, patrons, and cheerleaders. Also, make sure there are no other conflicting activities.
5. **Get your projects approved.** Check with your cheerleading coach first, then with your administration. Check with the school bookkeeper to find out school policy on purchase orders, financial records, and methods of handling and depositing money.
6. **Keep a file** on every project. Get organized! Make a checklist of exactly what has to be done, when, and by whom.
7. **Delegate duties** among squad members. Accurate records should be kept by each person in charge of an area.
8. **Organize your advertising and publicity.**
9. **Finalize all plans** right before the event. Check to see that everyone is prepared, knows when and where to meet, what to wear, and what to bring.
10. **Make sure the event runs smoothly.** Stay relaxed, friendly, enthusiastic, and personable with your customers and each other.

11. **Remember the importance of follow-through** once the project is over. Return borrowed items, clean up the area, write thank-you notes, do all accounting, record final results, and evaluate the project.

Here are some fund-raising ideas that should help solve your money problems:

1. **Surprise Packages**—gather together as many spirit-raising items as you can(antenna toppers, pennants, buttons, decals, etc.). Make up surprise packages (be sure to wrap them) and sell them to students. Don't tell them what's inside, and try to put different things in every package.

2. **Sidewalk Sweep**—talk with merchants around your town and see if you can sweep their walks before or after school for a fee.

3. **Rake Leaves During the Fall**—on a given weekend, gather together all members of your squad and go from door to door offering to rake leaves for a fee.

4. **Coat Check**—at basketball games and wrestling meets, set up a coat-check stand. People will appreciate this, and you can make good money.

5. **Shovel Snow**—during the winter go from house to house shoveling snow for a fee.

6. **Dig Dandelions**—during the summer go from door to door offering to dig dandelions for a fee.

7. **Stage a Walkathon**—get sponsors to pay you ten cents for each mile you walk to help boost school spirit.

8. **Hold an Auction or Garage Sale**—go from house to house asking people for things they would like to get rid of (pots, pans, dishes—anything) and then hold an auction or garage sale.

9. **Sell Potted Plants**—go to a local nursery and purchase quantities of small potted plants. Hold a garden or plant sale at your school or go from house to house selling them.

10. **Wash Windows at Drive-Ins**—you'll be surprised at how much money you can raise by offering to wash car windows as people arrive at drive-in movies.

11. **Rent Blankets**—at cold football games, have a supply of blankets handy and rent them to spectators.

12. **Prettiest Baby Contest**—get baby pictures of your athletes and hang them in the hall with a jar beneath each. Students will vote for the "prettiest baby" by putting money into the jars. Announce the winner at a pep rally.

13. **Egg Sale**—go to a house and ask for an egg . . . then go next door and sell them the egg. Be sure to tell people when their next-door neighbor contributes.

14. **Ugly Legs Contest**—take pictures of your athletes' legs and hang them in the hall with a jar beneath each picture. Students will vote with money for the ugliest legs. Announce the winner at a pep rally.

15. **Sell Any of the Following Items in Your School Colors or with Your School Name or Mascot Imprinted on Them:** class pins, decals, T-shirts, bumper stickers, license plates, plates, hats or stocking caps, scarves, kazoos, key chains, miniature footballs, buttons, cowbells, mini-mega-phones, patches, pennants, trash cans, helium-filled ballons, stuffed

animals or dolls of your mascot, book covers, pencils or pens, antenna toppers, student directories, mini-pompons, stadium cushions, confetti, stationery, mittens, shoe laces, football jerseys, painted rocks or beanbags.

16. **Set Up a Fresh Fruit or Vegetable Stand**—you can use magic markers to make your oranges look like basketballs, etc.

17. **Sell Any of the Following Food Items at School or at Athletic Events:** orange juice, soft drinks, popcorn balls, Cracker Jacks, potato chips, peanuts, bubble gum, ice cream, popsicles, submarine sandwiches, pizza, donuts, cupcakes, cinnamon rolls, cookies in the shape of footballs or basketballs, candied apples, brownies, cotton candy, cream puffs, jawbreakers, penny candy or watermelon slices.

18. **Bake Sale**—make cookies and ice them with students' first names. With this added "personal" touch you'll be surprised at how many of them you will sell.

19. **Odd-Job Day**—put an ad in your local newspaper advertising your services to the townspeople (ironing, babysitting, washing windows, etc.). Then hire yourselves out on weekends.

20. **Shoeshine Stand**—during your lunch period and after school, set up a shoeshine stand and charge a fee.

21. **Singing Telegrams**—you'll work with the athletes on this one. Any student who wishes to send a message to another student must pay for a telegram. Then one of the athletes has to deliver the message and sing it.

22. **Have a Feed**—after school or on a Saturday, hold some kind of a "feed." Serve chili, pancakes, pizza, etc. Charge a fee "per person."

23. **Have a Special Page in Your Football or Basketball Program**—entitle the page "We Support the Bears" (or the name of your team) and charge students and adults a fee to have their names listed.

24. **Rent a Movie and Charge Admission.**

25. **Raffle the Game Ball.**

26. **Babysit During P.T.A. Meetings.**

27. **Have a Cheerleading Clinic for Elementary Girls.**

28. **Have a Re-Cycled Can Drive.**

29. **Sell Carnations at Your Homecoming Game.**

30. **Form a Clean-up Committee After Halloween**—get your entire squad together and go from house to house offering to clean soap off windows, toilet paper out of trees, etc., for a fee.

31. **Sponsor a Hayride.**

32. **Hold a Class Penny-Jug Contest**—set up four one-gallon jars with slits in the top, and put them in the front hall of your school. Label each with either "freshmen," "sophomores," "juniors" or "seniors." Announce the contest to the school, pennies count "for" and silver coins (dimes, nickels, quarters, half-dollars) count "against." If you are senior, you will want to have all pennies in your jar and you'll put silver coins in the freshmen, sophomore and junior jars. Do this during a spirit week and award the winning class during a pep rally.

33. **Car Wash**—advertise in advance, have tickets printed and sell them door to door.

34. **Cheerleading Lessons**—set up a certain day after school to conduct private cheerleading lessons. Be sure to advertise in the paper.

35. **Sponsor a Talent Show, a Musical or Style Show, a Carnival or a**

Gymnastic Show—you could also present a "Gong Show" or a "Gay Nineties" night.

36. **Between Classes Set Up an "Emergency, 30-Second Massage Center"**—charge a fee and have all cheerleaders standing behind chairs ready to give 30-second shoulder massages.

37. **Penny Queen**—Three girls are selected from each class to run for "Penny Queen." Their pictures are put in the hall with a jar beneath each. Students vote by placing pennies into the jars. You might want to make this A "Mr. and Mrs. School Spirit Award" and announce the winners at a pep rally.

38. **Collect Pop Bottles**—go door to door and ask people if they will donate their empty pop bottles. Then turn them in for the deposits.

39. **School Tag Day**— station each cheerleader at a main intersection in town. Sell school tags that can be placed or stuck on car windows.

17

Pep Rally and Spirit Ideas

Your primary duty as a cheerleader is to raise and maintain school spirit. You can do this at your school through creative spirit-raising projects and effective, exciting pep rallies.

How you motivate your student body, as well as your crowd (which consists of your school faculty, your student body and their families), is a major responsibility. Unless a crowd is excited and enthusiastic they will not provide your athletes with the inspiration and support they need.

To make sure that you have an adequate spirit-raising program planned for the school year, you should begin organizing and planning during summer practice. Make a schedule of the major events at your school (such as homecoming, tournaments, rival games, etc.), which should include a spirit-raising event. List, also, the pep rallies and spirit weeks you want to stage (subject, of course, to approval by your principal).

Once you have compiled this information, decide on what type of spirit projects you want to hold—dances, inter-class competitions, etc.—and determine which school organizations and clubs you will involve. Remember that the more people you involve, the more successful your projects will be.

There are literally hundreds of different spirit-raising and pep rally ideas. Listed at the end of this chapter are some ideas that were created by cheerleaders just like you. After reading them, see how many different ideas you can create.

No matter what type of spirit-raising project or pep rally you conduct, remember that the key to its success is organization. Read the following guidelines, as they will help you in organizing and staging effective pep rallies:

1. Select dates for your rallies. Find out how many rallies you are allowed to have, check your game schedule and decide on which days you want to conduct rallies. Be sure to get the approval of your principal on your date selections.
2. Decide on the location of each rally. If you will be using any facilities other than the school gym, be sure to reserve them early. For variety you might use the auditorium and put on a real "show,"

using the curtains, special lighting, etc. Outdoor rallies, particularly bonfires, are exciting. If you do plan a bonfire, be sure to contact your local fire department so they can be standing by.

3. Decide what time of the day each rally will be held. The best time to hold a rally is during the last hour of school, but you can conduct them in the morning, during lunch hour or after school. When planning, remember that your rallies should never last more than thirty minutes. You don't want to bore your audience by dragging out the program.

4. Determine what props you may need other than microphones and/or record players. Special props are often needed for skits, spirit-raising chants or competitions. Costumes can usually be made or rented from a local costume store. Quite often only simple props, such as ladders, tables or chairs, are needed, but always use your imagination and be creative with your props.

5. Decide on a theme for each rally. Themes are generally centered around the opponents you face during the season, but there are hundreds of topics you can use as themes.

6. Determine what organizations, clubs, faculty, etc., you wish to involve in your rallies. You should try to include as many different people as possible. It becomes boring to an audience to see the same varsity cheerleaders performing cheers, chants and skits at every rally. You might try assigning one pep rally to each school club. That organization will then be responsible for performing a skit during their assigned rally. You should award a trophy for the best skit at the end of the year. Your athletes, class officers, faculty members, class "hams" can also be included in skits and competitions. The student body will begin to look forward to seeing who is going to be in the next rally.

7. Decide on the format of each rally. In order for each of your pep rallies to be effective, they must all be exciting and different. A standard rally consists of: 1) an entrance and opening; 2) one or two cheers; 3) spirit competitions; 4) a skit; 5) school fight song; 6) coach's talk and player introductions. Be sure to keep these hints in mind when planning your rallies:

   • Make your entrance flashy.
   • Always use music (either a loud and exciting pep band or recorded music over a P.A. system).
   • Keep announcements and directions brief and to the point. Do not announce each event of the rally.
   • Plan activity or music for every minute of the rally. Students tend to become critical when given time to do so, so keep the rally moving. You may want to use fun "commercials" between skits and cheers.
   • Tactfully ask your speakers to be brief.
   • Limit your rally to twenty to thirty minutes.

8. Decide how you want to advertise your rallies. You should constantly use new methods of advertising to stir up excitement and create interest. Any of the following methods can help you:

- Use the radio or newspaper.
- Post signs throughout the school.
- Have morning announcements over the intercom.
- Have two cheerleaders enter a classroom bouncing a basketball back and forth. They should carry on a brief conversation about the upcoming pep rally and game and leave the room without acknowledging that anyone was in it.
- Have a surprise rally the last hour of the day by sounding the fire alarm. Let everyone think it is a practice fire drill, but once the entire student body is outdoors, stage a pep rally. Be sure the fire department knows what you are planning, so they can either ignore the alarm or stage a practice drill of their own.

9. Figure out who will organize the cleanup, return of any borrowed props, etc., following your rallies.

Remember that the success of any pep rally or spirit-raising project depends on organization and creativity. Listed below are some ideas to get you started on your spirit-raising activities:

1. **Secret Spirit Pals.** Assign each cheerleader and pep club member one athlete. Throughout the season they are responsible for doing something for their "pal" and keeping it a secret. This can range from decorating his locker with victory signs, to giving him special "spirit food." A "spirit food" basket might include nuts (labeled "Go Nuts"), bananas (labeled "Go Bananas"), suckers (labeled "Lick 'em") or oranges (Orange you glad you're gonna' win?), etc. Be sure to have a friend deliver your basket so you can remain a "secret spirit pal."
2. **Spirit Sheets or Pillow Cases.** Buy sheets or pillowcases for each of your athletes and write spirit slogans on them (be sure to use laundry markers). The night before a big game, have the athlete's mother put the spirit sheets or pillowcases on his bed.
3. **Spirit Week.** Have a different theme for every day. Examples: Tacky Day—everyone must wear their tackiest clothes to school; Inside-Out Day—everyone has to wear their clothes inside out; Overall Spirit Day—everyone should show up wearing overalls; Top 'em Day—everyone must come to school wearing a hat; Stomp 'em Day—everyone should wear boots to school.
4. **Have Car Caravans to Away Games.**
5. **Silent Day**—no one is allowed to talk in the halls between classes, during lunch, etc., until the time of a giant pep rally, which is held at the end of the day.
6. **Set Up a Pep Rally Jail.** Set up your jail and arrest and jail people who aren't yelling during your rallies.
7. **Throw Miniature Footballs and Basketballs into the Stands When a Score is Made.**
8. **Post Signs Along the Route to Games.** Your signs should say such things as "You are entering Tiger Country," etc.
9. **Decorate Your School with Signs and Crepe Paper on the Morning of a Big Game.**

10. **Pajama Fashion Show.** Cheerleaders model the basketball and football players' pajamas during a rally.
11. **Have Your Faculty Dress Up as Cheerleaders and Lead Cheers at a Rally.**
12. **Decorate a Cake Like a Football Field.** Before a big game, deliver the cake to your football team.
13. **Decorate Each Player's Locker.**
14. **Have a "Meet the Team" Rally.** During the rally, let students meet the football players and talk to them about the upcoming game.
15. **Award a Free Game Pass.** Every week, you should give a free pass to the one member of the Pep Club who has shown exceptional spirit during the week.
16. **Have a Sign or Poster Contest.** Have a contest among the students to see who can make the best sign or poster depicting the game of the week. Give two free tickets to the winner.
17. **Competition yells.** These yells are the most effective spirit-raising tactics used during rallies. Any kind—student body against pep band and cheerleaders, one side of gym against the other, boys against girls, class against class, cheerleaders against team, etc. Tempt your audience with bubble gum (the louder they yell, the more gum you throw them). Hand out paper bags as students enter the gym and have the crowd pop them at the same time. Or have a whistling competition. Have a representative from each class receive a pie in the face, a dunking, etc., as a reward for their side yelling loudest.
18. **Have a Fifties Rally.** Everyone turns back the clock for this one. Students, cheerleaders and teachers dress in Fifties' clothes. Have the faculty lead a cheer from the Fifties and play Fifties' music during the rally.
19. **Off-Season Tug-of-War.** During the lull between football and basketball seasons, have a pep rally held for the purpose of arousing school spirit and showing that enthusiasm should not be confined just to the athletic field. Members of the cheerleading squad and pep club show up on one side of the gym floor wearing tennis shoes, shorts and sweatshirts. Members of the football team (same number as girls) show up wearing the same. The president of the student body produces a large rope and announces a tug-a-war. However, before the contest begins, the boys are required to take off their shoes and participate in their stocking feet. Of course, the girls will win because they have the necessary traction with their shoes.
20. **Commercials.** During pep rallies have various short commercials that will keep the audience's attention. For example: a cheerleader, wearing a grass skirt, runs across the gym floor five or six times at various intervals during the rally. Each time she runs across the floor, she is screaming at the top of her lungs. Finally, the last time she runs across the floor, a member of the football team is chasing her with a lawn mower.
21. **Dawn Dance:** At 6:30 A.M., have a dance and sell items such as donuts and orange juice.

22. **Come to Games in Different Kinds of Transportation.** Students should arrive in wagons, on bicycles, tricycles, scooters, skateboards, skates, etc.
23. **Backwards Day.** Everyone should appear at school wearing their clothes backwards, walking backwards, talking backwards.
24. **Have Your Teachers Do a Funny Skit.**
25. **Write a Giant Spirit Letter to Your Athletes.** The paper should be at least 4 feet by 5 feet and should read something like this: "Dear Players: We wanted to send you a SMALL note to say 'Good Luck' and to let you know we are behind you all the way. We have a tough school and a TOUGH team. If you'll give 110 percent, the cheerleaders will be right behind you giving 120 percent. Good Luck, EHS Cheerleaders."

18

Rules and Regulations

It is so important that your cheerleading squad operates under a specific set of rules so that you will effectively work as a team. Rules are written by the principal, the cheerleading sponsor, and the squad at the beginning of the year and are compiled in a constitution.

Your cheerleading constitution is a workable guide of values to follow during the year, an expression of your squad's beliefs and goals, and a guideline for all activities and functions involving the cheerleaders.

To give you an idea how rules are set up, read over the following sample cheerleader constitution:

Sample
EAST HIGH SCHOOL VARSITY CHEERLEADER CONSTITUTION
Basketball and Football Cheerleaders

I. PURPOSE

It shall be the purpose of this organization to promote and uphold school spirit, to develop good sportsmanship among students, to support athletic programs and to develop better relationships in the community and between schools during all athletic events. The organization goal is to work in harmony with the administration, faculty, band, athletic teams, and all other school organizations.

II. ELIGIBILITY REQUIREMENTS

A. A cheerleader candidate must be currently enrolled at East High School.

B. A candidate must be a rising junior or senior to be considered for varsity tryouts.

C. A candidate must have an overall "C" average with no "F" grades. (The guidance office will determine the eligibility of each candidate one week prior to tryout clinic. The standard method of class ranking will be used.)

D. Each candidate must turn in a written certification by a medical doctor stating she/he has passed a physical examination.

E. Each candidate must carry school accident insurance or present a signed waiver by parents stating they have adequate insurance.

F. Each candidate must turn in written parental permission form.

III. MEMBERSHIP

A. The East varsity squad will consist of 12 cheerleaders. The 13th score will be considered an alternate to be moved to a regular position in the event a vacancy occurs. The substitute will cheer in the event a regular cheerleader is unable to perform her cheerleading duties. The substitute will not dress in uniform unless he/she is scheduled to cheer.

    B. The entire cheerleading squad will cheer at all rallies, football games, and home basketball games. One half (6) cheerleaders will cheer at all away basketball games. Games will be assigned on a rotating basis.

IV. ATTENDANCE REQUIREMENTS (OTHER THAN GAMES)

    A. Summer clinic—All cheerleaders including the substitute are required to attend summer clinic. The sponsor only may excuse a cheerleader's attendance for illness or a family emergency. The manager is encouraged, but not required, to attend.

    B. Competition—The squad as a group will decide whether or not to enter a competition. If the majority vote to compete, the entire squad including the manager will attend.

    C. One-day clinic—The same rules apply as in competitions.

    D. Social activities—All members of the squad are encouraged, but not required, to attend. Advance notice is required from anyone not attending.

    E. Community activities—Each cheerleader is required to participate in three community activities a year. Certain community projects will be chosen by the squad and each cheerleader, manager, and sponsor is allowed to select the ones in which they wish to participate.

    F. If any other activities are chosen by the squad, the sponsor will decide if the event is optional or mandatory.

V. FINANCIAL RESPONSIBILITY (OTHER THAN UNIFORMS)

    A. Summer clinic—The cheerleader is responsible for cost of summer clinic. Fund-raising projects will be available for those who wish to participate.

    B. Summer clinic transportation—The school will be responsible for furnishing a bus, driver, and gas.

    C. Competitions and one-day clinics—The booster club will be responsible for any enrollment cost. The school will furnish transportation if the event is out of town. Any additional costs will be paid by the cheerleader.

    D. The school will furnish transportation to and from all out-of-town cheerleading activities.

    E. For out-of-town ballgames each cheerleader will receive the same food allotment that is given to the ball players.

    F. The cheerleader budget allows $200 for incidental spirit-raising activities. Any amounts outside this budget will be covered by the cheerleaders. A vote will be taken by the squad and permission must be granted by the sponsor for any extra expenditures.

VI. TRYOUTS

    A. The tryouts will consist of performing skills in front of a panel of judges (counting 60% of the total score) and before the student body (student body popular vote counting 30% of the total score). A teacher rating by five teachers (of the candidate's choice) will count 10% of the candidate's total score.

1. The judges will be chosen on the basis of their expertise in cheerleading. They will be selected from college cheerleaders and cheerleader sponsors outside East High's school district.
2. All skills will be graded on the basis of the level of perfected execution (highest score possible on each skill is 10 points).
3. Each candidate will be rated by five teachers on the basis of attendance, punctuality, and conduct observed in that class. Each candidate may earn a maximum of two points from each of the five teachers (total possible 10 points or 10% of the total score).
4. Cheerleader tryouts will be held annually during the first part of April.
5. All skills necessary to try out for varsity cheerleader will be taught at a tryout clinic conducted by the senior cheerleaders. This clinic will last one week and will be held two weeks prior to tryouts. Attendance 80% of the time at tryout clinic is mandatory.

VII. SELECTION OF CAPTAIN, CO-CAPTAIN, AND OTHER OFFICERS
   A. The varsity cheerleading squad will have one head captain and one co-captain. The sponsor will prepare a list of recommended candidates, then the squad will vote from the names on this list to make the final selection of the captains. The head captain must have a minimum of one year's experience on the varsity squad.
   B. The varsity cheerleading squad will have the following officers:
      1. Secretary—The captains and sponsor will select one cheerleader to act as secretary.
      2. Treasurer—The captains and sponsor will select one cheerleader to act as treasurer.
      3. Chaplain—The captains and sponsor will select one cheerleader to act as chaplain.
      4. Manager—The cheerleading squad will make nominations for a person to serve in this office. Also a sign-up list will be posted on the bulletin board for anyone interested to sign up. The squad will narrow the selection to three candidates, then the sponsors and captains will interview the candidates and make the final selection.

VIII. DUTIES AND RESPONSIBILITIES OF THE CAPTAIN AND OFFICERS
   A. The captain will be responsible for the following:
      1. Set an example for the rest of the squad by following all rules and regulations for the East High Cheerleaders. The captain will set an example by always being willing to do more than her share.
      2. Work closely with co-captain.
      3. Be at practice early and start practice on time.
      4. Take over practice and meetings in the absence of sponsor.
      5. Be responsible for contacting all cheerleaders to notify them of practice, change in plans, etc.
      6. Select cheers and chants to be used at games and rallies. The squad should make suggestions and the captain should definitely consider their suggestions, but the final decision is made by the captain.

7. Call for a vote in case of disagreement concerning squad decisions. Act as a peacemaker.
8. Be responsible for greeting visiting cheerleaders before the start of a game. Arrange with manager for half-time refreshments. Inform visiting captain of plans.
9. Coordinate painting and hanging up of signs.
10. Select (with input from squad) the uniforms to be worn at all cheerleading events. Distribute in writing a list of complete uniforms to be worn for the entire week (at least 3 days in advance, no last-minute changes).
11. Keep an accurate record of all attendance and tardies, and turn these records in to the sponsor every Monday.
12. Organize pep rallies with sponsor, band director, and coaches.
13. Coordinate spirit-raising activities, getting sponsor and coaches approval in advance.
14. Keep the crowd cheering during a game. Idleness is not acceptable.
15. Keep the cheerleaders in proper formation at games.
16. Show no partiality within the squad.
17. Bring problems to the sponsor so she may help the squad run smoothly.
18. In the event the captain is not able to perform her duties the co-captain will take over until she is able to resume the duties.
19. During basketball season, when the squad is divided into two groups, the captain and co-captain shall be equal and each in complete charge of one group.

B. The officers of the squad will be responsible for the following:
1. Secretary
   a. Write welcome notes to all visiting squads.
   b. Write thank-you notes whenever necessary.
   c. Order any gifts when deemed appropriate (must have sponsor approval).
   d. Handle all written correspondence.
2. Treasurer
   a. Assist the sponsor in collecting money.
   b. Assist the sponsor in record-keeping of money.
   c. Make deposits to the office bookkeeper.
   d. Prepare a written report (monthly) showing financial standing of the squad. Present this information to the squad each month.
3. Chaplain
   a. In charge of prayer prior to cheerleading activities.
   b. Arrange annual church visit as a group.
   c. Represent the squad in any religious matters.
4. Manager
   a. Take charge of all equipment.
   b. Take charge of hanging and removing of signs.
   c. Attend all games and rallies.
   d. In charge of first-aid supplies, having supplies at every game, and replenishing when necessary.
   e. Take charge of providing refreshments for visitors at home games.

IX. PRACTICE SCHEDULE
   A. Number of practices to be held
      1. Last six weeks of school
         a. Twice a week
      2. Summer
         a. Three weeks prior to camp—3 times a week
         b. Two weeks prior to camp—daily
         c. One week prior to camp—daily, if necessary
         d. One week prior to beginning of school—daily
   B. Each practice will last 1½ to 2 hours
   C. During school practice will start at 3:30 P.M. During the summer the days and time will be selected by the squad.
   D. All cheerleaders are required to attend all practices.
   E. Only the sponsor has the authority to excuse a cheerleader from practice. Excuses will be granted only in the case of illness or emergencies. Make all routine dental and doctor appointments around scheduled practices.

X. TRANSPORTATION
   A. Home or local games
      1. The cheerleader is responsible for securing transportation for all games.
      2. Away games
         A. The sponsor will arrange transportation on the school bus or, if a bus is not available, the cheerleaders will ride in a car driven by parents or a qualified adult as approved by the principal.
         B. All cheerleaders will return by the same transportation unless the parents notify the sponsor personally or by written note that the parents agree to and accept responsibility for the change in transportation.

XI. PURCHASE AND CARE OF UNIFORMS
   A. The school will make original purchase of all uniforms. This includes skirts, sweaters, dress-type uniforms, and pompons. All items purchased by the school remain school property.
   B. The cheerleader is responsible for purchasing all practice or camp uniforms, blouses, tights, socks, shoes, letters for sweaters, and jackets.
   C. The cheerleading squad is responsible for additional uniforms (i.e., if squad size increases), any alterations or necessary upkeep on uniforms. THE SPONSOR AND THE CHEERLEADER SQUAD WILL SELECT STYLE OF ALL UNIFORMS THEY ORDER SUBJECT TO APPROVAL OF PRINCIPAL.
   D. Cheerleader jackets and T shirts are the *ONLY* part of the cheerleader's uniform that may be worn when not in complete uniform or not at a cheerleader function. The only jacket that can be worn over a cheerleader uniform is the official cheerleader jacket.
   E. All school uniforms must be cleaned (by cleaners) and returned one week from the date of the last event. Any uniform that is damaged and deemed unusable by the sponsor must be paid for at replacement.

XII. APPEARANCE
   A. Uniforms—Uniforms and shoes will be kept spotlessly clean at

all times. Uniforms must be neatly pressed and not in need of mending.

    B. Jewelry—It is recommended that no jewelry be worn while cheering. A small pair of post earrings and small, flat rings may be worn. No other jewelry is allowed.

    C. Make up—No excessive makeup. A natural wholesome look is the one desired; any girl wearing too much makeup while wearing the cheerleading uniform will be required to remove it. Makeup must pass the approval of the sponsor.

    D. Hair Styles—All hair styles must be neat and out of the face. It should be a simple style for cheering and not require any attention (combing etc.) while performing.

    E. A cheerleader should look her best physically at all times. Maintaining proper weight will keep a cheerleader performance and appearance at their peak.

XIII. AWARDS

    A. Spirit Award—The cheerleader sponsor will select the person she believes has demonstrated the best spirit (both inner spirit and the outward show of pep and spirit) during the entire year.

    B. Most Outstanding Cheerleader—The cheerleader squad will select the person on the squad that has been the best cheerleader during the entire year.

XIV. FUND-RAISING ACTIVITIES

    A. All cheerleaders will participate in the first fund-raising project of the year. This money will be used to fund all miscellaneous expenses needed during the year (i.e., paint, ink, tape, surprises for team, etc.)

    B. Fund-raising projects will be arranged for camp expenses and personal items needed for the uniform. Any girl who wishes may earn all or part of the money needed to cover these items. Two projects (choice of squad) will be held for personal needs of cheerleaders. A parent who wishes to pay for all clinic expenses and personal items of the uniform must do so before school is out for the summer. All fund raising will be completed before school is out.

    C. Before any fund-raising activity is approved, plans for the use of the profits will be on file with the principal.

XV. GAME OR RALLY SUSPENSION

    A. Grades—Any six-weeks F will result in suspension from the squad until this grade is raised to passing. Grades will be rechecked at the end of a two-week period, and weekly intervals thereafter to check for progress. The minimum time docked or suspended for grades is two weeks.

    B. Suspension from school—If a cheerleader is suspended from school for an infraction of school rules, she will be suspended from the squad for a period of no less than two weeks. Length of time decided by the sponsor and principal depending on the seriousness of the situation.

    C. Suspension from game and rally

       1. A cheerleader may be suspended from participating at games, pep rallies, or any other cheerleading activity for any of the following reasons:

         a. Unexcused absence from any cheerleading activity

        b. Excessive tardies to cheerleading activity

        c. Failure to do assigned cheerleading duties

        d. Failure to abide by cheerleading rules and regulations

        e. Failure to cooperate with squad and/or sponsor or administration

        f. Not attending cheerleading activity on false pretense (i.e., faking illness—absences from all cheerleading activities will be checked by the sponsor)

  2. If a cheerleader misses practice and it is unexcused, this will result in suspension from 1st ballgame or pep rally—whichever comes first. Second unexcused practice—removal from squad. Excuses are left to the discretion of the sponsor. Any time a practice is missed, it must be cleared ahead of time. If you cannot contact the sponsor, contact the head cheerleader; she will relay the message to the sponsor—she will not have the authority to excuse the absence.

        a. Minor disciplinary problems or tardies

            1. 1st time—no penalty

            2. 2nd time—discretion of the sponsor (i.e, paint signs, organize supply room, etc.)

            3. 3rd time—miss 1st pep rally or ball game

            4. 4th time—miss 1 rally and 1 game or 2 games (REQUIRED PARENT CONFERENCE AT THIS TIME)

            5. 5th time—removal from squad

            EXAMPLE: late two times and not working 100% at practice. This is three disciplinary situations—miss one pep rally or game.

            TARDY: A tardy consists of not being at the designated area, ready for whatever activity involved, within five (5) minutes of the stated time.

  D. Attendance requirements during suspension from squad

    1. Practice—required to attend all practice sessions

    2. Pep rallies—required to attend

    3. Games—attendance requested, but not required

XVI. DISMISSAL

  A. Offenses that result in dismissal

    1. Accumulation of five minor disciplinary problems or tardies

    2. The second F made on the report card

    3. Unbecoming conduct (use of drugs, alcohol, stealing, being jailed for any reason, etc.) which reflects on the reputation of the school or the cheerleading squad

    4. Repeated insubordination toward sponsor, captain, or any school personnel

  B. Tryout eligibility or cheerleader that is dismissed or resigns

    1. A cheerleader will be considered eligible to try out for cheerleader one year from the date of dismissal or resignation. The reason for dismissal will not have any adverse effect on future tryouts if the problem has been corrected and has not been repeated during the year.

19

A Gallery of Cheers and Chants

General Use Cheers

Break

Break away
Move ahead
We're breakin' away
Break away!

Defense

Defense Eagles
Push that team aside
Get in gear and go team
Get the winning stride!

Power

Eagles oh yes
We've got the power
yes the best
power we've got
Hot!
Power we've got
Hot!!

Hey

Hey! ICF! Hey!
Will be number one
Hey we are the best
Hey!!

Eagles

Eagles Eagles
Eagles take control
Attack! Attack!!
Attack fight back!!!

Alive

Alive with power
Eagles will conquer
Rise to the top Eagles win!

Time

The time is right
For a victory tonight
Eagle team!
Fight team!!

Score

Score big
Score more
Score now
S-C-O-R-E
Score big
Score more
Score now!

Eagles Hold That Line

Eagles hold that line
Hold it one more time
It's fourth down
Let's turn it around
Eagles hold that line!

Gotta Work

Eagles you gotta work
Gotta Work
Work
Work
Eagles you gotta work
You gotta take that ball on
   in
Eagles work
Eagles win
Eagles take it in!

Beat It

B-E-A-T Beat it!
Turkey team
B-E-A-T BEAT IT!
'Cause we're mean!

Let's Fight

Block 'em Stomp 'em
Whip those turkeys right
Block 'em Stomp 'em
Let's fight!

Go Let's Go

Go, let's go
Offense move that ball!
Go, let's go
Eagles take it all!!

Step Up

Step up to fight
Step up to win
Eagle team XX dig in!

Hello

Eagles say "Hello"
H-e-l-l-o
From us to you
A welcome too
Eagles say hello!

We're Making It

We're making it all the way
We're on the top to stay
We're making it move
Eagles making it move!

Hey Eagles

Hey Eagles
Shout your name
Say Eagles
"Eagles!"
Who's gonna win the game?
Say Eagles
"Eagles!"
Eagles shout your name!
(Repeat)

Eagles Doing It Right

Eagles doing it right
We're gonna win this game
   tonight

You gotta do it good
You gotta do it right
Eagles win tonight!

Hit 'em Hard

Eagles hit 'em hard
Eagles gain that yard
and—hit 'em hard!

Rise

Eagle team will rise
Take you by surprise
We're on our winning
   course
Fear the Eagle force!

Slam

Slam! Attack!
That's the name of this
   game
Intimidate, Don't hesitate
Shout the Eagle name!

Score

Eagles! Eagles!
Take control of this game
S-C-O-R-E score, We want
   more!

Command

Get over it!
Eagles have command
Jump back! You'll see
Eagle Territory!

Dominate

Dominate Eagles
I C F take charge
Go! Fight!
Victory in sight!

With It

Get with it
Stick with it
We're out to get that team

Get with it
Stick with it
Eagle team (XX)
Get mean!

Victory

Go Fight!
Victory tonight
Victory tonight eagles
Go let's fight

Shout

Eagles fans lets shout
We're #1(XXX)
The word is out

Beware

This is our year
To dominate, devastate
A championship is near
1-2-3
Watch us you will see
That the mighty Eagle team
Will have a victory
We're dominating,
   devastating
(XXX) Beware!!!

Charge

Watch out (X) Tigers
(step clap clap)
We're taking charge
You can't compete
With our winning streak
Our mighty power
Will defeat
So stand (X) Behind
Hold fast that line (XXX)
Watch out Tigers (XXX)
WE're taking charge!

Power to Win

We've got the power
To win tonight
So come on team
Let's fight!
Power team, Fight
Win tonight! HEY!

Conquer

We'll conquer
The world
In a minute or two
But first we're gonna
Do it to you!

Pride

We've got pride
PRIDE
Got Pride
Eagles have pride
Blue pride

Do It

We've got to do it
Go ahead
Prove it
Eagles can do it

Can You Do It?

Can you do it?
Yea, we can do it!
But can you do it?
Yea, we can do it!
What are you going to do?
Beat, beat South
Beat South

Gonna Make It

We're gonna make it
'Cause the Eagles can take
   it
They're rough, they're tough
They're mean enough
Mighty Eagles show your
   stuff
Eagles gonna make it!

Hit It

Hey, hit it
Eagles
I said hit it
You're with it
I said hit it!

Succeed

Onward Eagles to victory
We shall succeed
We shall succeed!

Get That Ball

Get that ball
And go
Don't move slow
Get that ball and
GO!

Strive for Success

Strive for success
Eagles reign
Over all the rest
Strive for success!

Victory Bound

Victory Bound
Eagle team
Can be found.
They're the ones
That're victory bound!

Stop 'em

STOP
Stop 'em, stop 'em
Top 'em!

Shout

You'll know we're Eagles
Without a doubt
Listen to the Eagle fans
   shout
EAGLES
(clap) Eagles!

The Best

Eagles are the best
We can surpass any test
Travel far, see the rest
Eagles rate
The BEST!

On the Move

The Eagle team
Is on the move
The team that always
Will pull through
Eagles on the move!

Victory Spot

Eagles, fight
With all you've got
Hit the vitory spot
Win again!

Take Hold

Take hold!
Rule,
Dominate!
Get tough,
Move!
Eagles, great!

Number One

Our team is first
We're second to none
Eagles best (clap, clap)
Number one!

Spirit and Might

We possess
Spirit and might
We can't be beat
So go team
FIGHT!

Hit 'em Harder

Hit 'em harder, Eagles
Don't stop!
Keep on fighting, Eagles
Unitl you reach the top
Don't stop!

Fight

Fight a little harder
Hold that line
Push 'em back
One more time
Fight!

It's Up to You

Over, under
Around and through
It's up to you
Mighty Eagles
Break through!

Reach the Top

Forward, onward
Eagles reach the top
Workin' for a victory
Don't stop!

Much More Spirit

Spirit, spirit, hey
We need more!
Much more spirit
MUCH MORE!!!

Eagles, Fight

Eagles, fight!
There's a job to be done
A game to be won
Eagles, fight
Make it
Victory, tonight!

Shine

We'll shine you on
You can't do right
You've got no spirit
You've got no fight
We'll shine you on!

Get it Together

Get it together
Strike a lead
We've got the spirit
That our team needs
Ah, get it
TOGETHER!

Action

Action, Eagles
We want to see you fight
Action, Eagles

We want to see your might
Action, Eagles!

Fight Until the End

Fight until the end
Until we win
No matter what it takes
Keep fighting
For victory's sake
Fight until the end
Eagles win!

Ready to Go

Eagles are ready
To go
Forward, onward
Let's go
Eagles on top, never stop!

Beat 'em

Beat 'em, beat 'em
We must defeat 'em
Go . . . beat 'em
Fight . . . beat 'em
Beat 'em
Defeat 'em!

Watchout

Determination, ability
Eagles are after a victory
Hey, Bears
Watchout!

Fight for It

Eagles!
Fight for it!
Hit 'em with
All you've got
Get the ball
Don't stop
Fight for it!

Got Spirit

Got spirit
Eagle spirit
Let's hear it
EAGLES

Eagle spirit, let's hear it
Victory we shall see
Give 'em Eagle spirit!

Eagle Pride

Eagle pride is on the move
Eagle team will never lose
(seven claps)
EAGLES!

Good Word

The good word is here to
   say
We'll back the Eagles all the
   way
Eagles!

Extra, Extra

Extra, Extra
That's our team
Extra fast
With lots of steam
Extra special team!

Just Begun

The Eagle team has just
   begun
We will be rated
NUMBER ONE!

Destroy

Destroy
Conquer
Leave 'em in the past
The mighty Eagles are the
   ones
That'll last!

Work It Out

Strike fast, hit hard
Get control now
Work it out
Run 'em down
Get that victory crown!

Spirit

Let's spell spirit
As loud as we can
Let's spell spirit
Like loyal fans
SPIRIT

Without a Doubt

Without a doubt
Eagles will shout
The loudest
And fight the hardest
Without a doubt
The Eagles will win!

Hey

Hey, hey
Hey you, Eagles
Go . . . fight . . . win!

Strive to Win

Strive to win!
Never give in
GO, FIGHT, WIN!

Ain't Bad

We ain't bad
'Cause we know we're good
Gonna walk on the Vikings
Like we walk on wood
Get up, get down, all
  around
Get down!

Get with It

With plenty of might
And lots of fight
Eagles
Get with it!

Stand Up

Stand up
For your team
And yell real loud
Eagles need support
From the loyal crowd
STAND UP!

On Top

Up there, on top
Eagles don't stop
Always go
Never stop
Eagle team
Reach the top!

Courage and Might

Hear us in our call
Raiders you will fall
Our team is a wall
Of courage and might
Eagles have courage
Watch them fight!

Power

Eagles talk of power
Power is what we've got
When we use our power
We're on top!

Beam 'Em

It's got to be
A victory!
Beat 'em!

Work to Win

Eagles . . . work to win
Now's the time to begin
Work as hard as you can
Take a victory stand
Let's begin
Work to win!

Determination

Determination
Pushes us on
Determination
Makes us strong
Team inspiration
is our determination!

Mighty Fightin'

Do it, Eagles
Win!
Mighty Fightin' Eagles
Do it, again!

We're Ready

Our team is rough
Our team is tough
We're ready!

Action, Speed

Ok, hey!
Action, action
Speed, speed
Hey team, it's what we need
ACTION
We want action!

On the Go

Eagles are on the go
No one can stop us
No one can top us
We're ready to go
Eagles are on
The go!

Eagles Will Fight

Eagles will fight
With all their might
The Eagles will win
A triumph
Again!

Fire Up

Fire up
Spark your spirit
Put on the heater
Show those Bears
We can't be beat
Hey, Eagles
Fire up!

Proud We Are

Proud we are
Success is ours
And spirit our guide
For we possess
Tiger pride
PROUD WE ARE!

Won't Let Us Down

Eagles, Eagles
is our name
We've got the boys
That'll win this game
So come on, team
Go to town
Eagle boys
Won't let us down

When You're Up

When you're up, you're up
When you're down, you're
    down
When you're up against the
    Eagles
You're upside down!

Victory Spirit

It's a cinch
That we will win
With the victory spirit
Our team is in
Lead the way,
Big team
Victory: BEGIN . . .

Hello Cheer

Now is the time
This is the way
To give you a greeting in a
    special way
HELLO
Central says HELLO!

Championship Cheer

We've got the pep
We've got the zip!

We are out for the
    Championship!
We've got the boys
And the best team yet
Will we win it?
YOU BET!!!

Eagles Strong

Our spirit is mounting
The crowd is counting
The minutes until we win
Go, fight, win!!!

Very Best Team

The Eagles are rough
The Eagles are mean
The Eagles are the
Very best team
EAGLES
The very best team!

Get That Ball

Get that ball!
Get that ball!
Score, score
Eagles, fight
With strength and might
Score, score, score!

Fight Harder

We fight harder
Every game we play
We fight harder
To bring a victory our way
Eagles fight harder!

Mighty Eagles

Mighty, mighty
Mighty, mighty Eagles
Go, fight, win!
Mighty, mighty
Mighty, fightin' Eagles
Win, win, win!

Go, Go, Beat, Beat

Go, go
Beat, beat
Never, never
Meet defeat
Go, go
Fight, fight
Win, win . . .
TONIGHT!

We've Got Pride

We've got pride on
Our side
You know it (Clap, Clap)
We show it (Clap, Clap)
WE'VE GOT PRIDE!

Above, Beyond

Above, beyond
We always seek
Reach, surpass
Our highest peak,
Above, beyond
Eagles strong!

Good Luck

The Eagles and the Trojans
Are going to fight
May the best team win
This game tonight
We meet you,
We greet you . . .
GOOD LUCK!

Proud

We're Eagles
And we're PROUD
Shout it loud . . .
PROUD!

All Right

Come on, Eagles
Work it out right
I said come on, Eagles
Let's go (Clap, Clap)
Let's fight (Clap, Clap)
ALL RIGHT!

Welcome Varsity

We've got the team that's
    really tough
So here's our varsity
Rough, tough, VARSITY!

Get It Together

Get it together
Eagles . . .
And get it done!
WIN!

Meet the Test

We are the Eagles
And we are the best!
Eagles meet the test!

Spirit

Hey . . . you
Out in the crowd!
If you've got that spirit
Then clap out loud
(ten claps)
HEY!

Victory Bound

We've got the . . .
Pride
Spirit
And energy
Victory bound!

Retaliate

Don't give up
We are great!
Courage, strength
RETALIATE!

Welcome Cheer

We're the Eagles and we're
Proud of our school!
We're the Eagles and we
Welcome you!

Hustle and Fight

Eagles!
Hustle and fight!
Win . . . do it right!

Victory Now

Eagles supreme
In every way
Victory now
Is what we say,
VICTORY NOW!

Pride

We can't hide
Our Eagle pride
Blue and Gold
SCORE!

Don't Give Up

Don't give up
Blue and Gold
Don't give in!
Fight, Eagles . . .
FIGHT . . .
AND WIN!!

Victory Spell Out

Don't hide
Your Eagle pride
Hear our cry!
V(V)
I(I)
C(C)
T(T)
O(O)
R(R)
Y(Y)

Get Ready

Get ready to go
Get ready to fight
Get ready you Eagles
We're winning tonight
Go, fight, win tonight!
HEY!

On the Move

Eagles are
On the move
We will fight
We will prove
That we're the best
Eagles on the move!!

Get to It

Mighty fightin' Eagles
We can do it
So let's get to it
Eagles get to it!

Road to Victory

For the Eagles
It's plain to see
We're on the road
To victory
Eagle victory!!

Shout

Let's shout for the blue
Let's shout for the gold
Let's shout for our team
They'll never fold
Shout . . . HEY!

Up with Victory

Up with victory
down with defeat
Central Eagles
Won't be beat!!!

Action, Speed

Action, speed, in the lead
Central High School
Will succeed!!

Teamwork

Teamwork, Eagles
Together we can work
For victory
T E A M work
Teamwork . . .
Eagles have it!

Blue, White, Fight

Blue . . . White . . . fight
VICTORY
Victory tonight . . .
FIGHT!

Pull for Team

We're gonna pull for our
   team,
We're gonna show you what
   we mean
Watch out!
We're pulling for our team!

Defense, Eagles

Defense, Eagles,
Hold 'em, hold 'em strong
Defense, Eagles
Hold 'em tight,
Hold 'em long
Hold 'em!!

Go Get 'em

Go, go, get 'em, get 'em
Fight, fight
Hit 'em, hit 'em
Win, win
Go, fight, win!

Watchout

Watchout, Trojans
Keep your heads up high
The mighty Eagles
Are passing by!
(XX XX)
Watchout!

Never Give In

Fight, Eagles, fight
Never give in
Fight, Eagles, fight
We've got to win!

Stand for Victory

Eagle pride is victory bound
Eagles are the best team all
   around
We will win
Wait and see . . .
Eagles stand for victory!

Best in the Land

The Eagles are ready
They've made their stand
They'll conquer all others
They're best in the land!

Eagles are Best

The Eagles are best
Without a doubt
Watch the team
And hear us shout . . .
Eagles, Eagles, Eagles!

Back to Win

Keep up the spirit
Don't give in!
The Eagles are moving
Back to win!

Defeat

The Eagles just can't be
   beat
They always cry defeat
The Eagles . . .
Can't be beat!

Roarin' to Win

Eagle spirit never gives in
Because the Eagles are
   roarin' to win
We're behind our team
We really scream
EAGLES WIN!

Fight to the End

Success is our goal
We'll fight to the end
Be on your guard
The Eagles will win!

Got to Score

Go Eagles . . .
We need more
Go Eagles . . .
We've got to score! GO!

Fight Back

Fight back, Eagles
Don't give in
Fight back, Eagles
We've got to win
Fight, Eagles!

Aim High

Aim high, Eagles
Reach the sky!
The Blue and Gold are
   victory bound
Eagles are the best team
   (XX) all around
Aim high, Eagles!

Won't Take Defeat

The Eagles are winning
They can't be beat!
They'll fight with all their
   might
They won't take defeat
Go, fight, win . . .
EAGLES!

On Attack

The Eagles are attacking
They won't hold back
Trojans better watch out . . .
Eagles are on attack!

Slip By

Watch out, Trojans
Keep your guard up high
Or the mighty Eagles
Will slip right by
Watchout!

Meet Any Test

Beware of the Eagles
They'll meet any test
Beware of the Eagles
'Cause they're the best!
Beware!

Reach for the Sky

Go, Eagles, reach for the
    sky
We'll stand behind you
And watch you fly . . .
Eagles reach . . .
For the sky!

Win Tonight

Eagles will fight
With all of their might . . .
And win tonight!

Light the Fire

Eagles,
Light the fire
Take us
SCORE!

Eagle Might

The Eagles will win
Without much fight
To show the Trojans
All their might . . .
Eagles!

The Best

Trojans think they're great
But never the less . . .
Eagles know different
'Cause they're the best
Eagles!

Winning

The Eagles are winning
They can't be beat
They'll fight with all their
    might!
They won't take defeat!

Beat

B-E-A-T Beat the Vikings
Beat the Vikings, hey!
Beat those Vikes!

Spell-Out Cheer

V-I-C-T-O-R-Y
Eagles fight, Eagles try
S-C-O-R-E
Eagles get a victory!

Might

Go, Eagles, go
Show 'em your might!
Eagles are the best,
Fight . . . fight . . . fight!

Football Cheers

Down the Field

Our team is making tracks
They're moving down the
    field
The Eagle team won't yield
MOVE IT DOWN THE
    FIELD!

For The Eagles

For the Eagles
It's never too late
We'll march down the field
We'll show them we're great
Eagles
Are great!

Seven Points More

We know
Which way to go
Under the goal post
Over the top
Seven points more, Eagles
Never stop

Rule for Force

Conquer the Raiders
Rule by force!
Take over the field
Lead the course!
Conquer the Raiders!

Fight

Fight a little harder
Hold that line
Push 'em back
Another time!
Fight hard,
Eagles
FIGHT!

Hit Hard

To make that score go
Higher, higher
We've got to hit 'em
Harder, harder
Hit hard, Eagles
Mow 'em down!

Rally Up

Rally up!
Get moving,
See that score
Make another touchdown,
We want more!
Rally up!

Rough Bears

Rough Bears, FIGHT
Tough Bears, FIGHT
Rough Bears (clap, clap)
Tough Bears (clap, clap)
FIGHT (clap, clap)
BEARS (clap, clap) FIGHT!

Let's Go Over

Let's go over
Between the goalposts
  send it
Let's go over
Push forward, defend it
Over Eagles
Six more!

Touchdown

Down that field
Raise that score!
Eagle team, give us more
Touchdown, Eagles
TOUCHDOWN!

Cross That Line

Get the ball, Eagles
And cross that line
Make that six-point run
Another time!
Cross that line
Another time!
SCORE!

Rough, Tough

Rough, tough Eagles
Pushing for a touchdown
Hey, fight
Rough, tough Eagles
Win tonight!

Eagles Will Win

Eagles will win
And win again
The Eagle team
Will win!!

Charge On

Down the field
Charge on
Over the line

Be strong
C H A R G E
Run 'em down
CHARGE ON!

Six Points More

It's a snap
We'll fill the gap
Ready to score
Six points more . . .
HEY!

Breakthrough

Eagles
Breakthrough!
It's up to you
Run over the line
Another time!
Breakthbrough!

Hold 'em

Hold 'em
S T O P
Stop 'em
Hold 'em where they are
H O L D
Hold 'em
Don't let 'em get too far
Hold 'em, stop 'em, top
  'em!

Take Over

Eagles
Take over!
Get the upper hand
Take a stand
Eagles
Take over
Take six!!

Gonna Make It

We're gonna make it
Cause the Eagles can take
  it
They're rough
They're tough
Mighty Eagle team gonna
Show their stuff
Eagles gonna make it
TOUCHDOWN

On the Top

On the top
On the bottom
In the middle
On the side
When you're messing with
  the Eagles
Better run and hide!

Put It Through

Over, under
Around and through
Come on, kicker
Put it through
Field goal!

Get That Ball

Get that ball
And go!
Down the field
Do not yield
GO, GO, GO!

Take a Stand

Eagles!
Take over . . .
Get the upper hand
Take a stand!
Eagles . . . take six!

Spirit and Might

We possess
Spirit and might!
We can't be beat
So hit 'em with the spirit,
Hit 'em with the might!
Come on, mighty
  Eagles . . . fight!

Onward

Onward to the goalpost
Eagles strive to win
T O U C H D O W N
Onward to win
TOUCHDOWN

Stop and Watch

Stop
And watch the Eagles
As they charge down the
   field
Stop
And watch the Eagles
   charge
Eagles will score
Fight some more
Stop and watch!

Gotta Move

Eagles
Gotta move
To prove
We got it
Move, Eagles
Down the field
Gotta move!

Touchdown Pass

Eagles are
Alert and fast
Ready for that
Touchdown pass
Touchdown!

Keep on Movin'

Keep on movin'
Down the field
Very fast
Run, pass
Keep on movin!

Number One

The Eagles . . .
Are coming out!
Number one!
We're on the run!
YOU CAN'T STOP US NOW!

Hold That Line

Hold that line
Hit 'em hard
Make 'em fight

For every yard
Eagles
Hold that line!

Can Do It

We can do it
Go ahead and prove it
Eagles
Can do it . . .
   TOUCHDOWN!

We'll Get Ya

We'll get ya
The Eagles will give you a
   scare
We'll get ya
So Trojans you better
   beware
The Eagles
Will get ya!

Hey, Spirit

Hey, spirit,
We need more!
Hey, team
Raise that score!
Spirit, score . . . give us
   more!
HEY, SPIRIT!

Eagle Pride

Eagle pride
P R I D E
Eagle pride
On our side . . .
Hey!

Don't Mess Around

Eagles . . .
Knock those Bears
Right on the ground!
'Cause . . . we . . .
WE DON'T MESS AROUND!

Conquer

Eagles conquer!
Lead the victory march
Down the field . . .
Over the goal . . .
Come on, Eagles,
Conquer!

Win Tonight

Win tonight
We want a win tonight!
Do it, Eagles
Fight . . .
Win . . .
Tonight!

The Time Is Now

The time is now
So go . . .
Hit high . . .
Hit low . . .
The time is now . . . SO GO!

Get It

GO!
GO!
Get-that-ball
Go-down-the field
Get it!
And GO!

Got What It Takes

The Eagle team
Has got what it takes
Our boys on the field
Won't give you a break
The Eagles . . .
Have got what it takes!

Make That Point

Hey, Eagles
Hear our call!
Let's see you really
Kick that ball . . .
Make that point!
Hey, hey!

Basketball Cheers

Jump, Team

Jump, team
And make a basket
Two points more
Come on and score!
Jump, team and score!

Hey, Spirit

Hey, spirit (clap, clap)
We need more
Hey, team (clap, clap)
Raise that score
Basket!

Flyin' High

Flyin' high
Up to the sky
Eagle team
Can't be denied
Flyin' high!

Basket Score

We want a basket
Raise that score
We've got 88
But we want more!
Basket, basket
Team, score!

Two Points More

It's a snap
We'll fill the gap
Ready to score
Two points more
Score, score
Raise it!

Spirit Roar

Lightening flash! (clap,
   clap, clap)
Spirit roar! (clap, clap, clap)
The Pioneers are on the
   floor!

1-2-3-4

1-2-3-4
Move that ball right down
   the floor
(clap, clap)
Stomp 'em, Knights, stomp
   'em!

We Want a Basket

We want a basket
Just two more
So come on, Eagles
Let's score!

What You Say

What you say?
Beat 'em!
What you say?
Defeat 'em!
What you say?
Beat 'em, defeat 'em . . .
   let's go!

Stay Calm

Stay calm, Big George
We're with you!
Score two more,
   George . . .
We're all with you!

Down the Floor

Down the floor
Raise that score!
Make it, make it!
Two more!

Steal It

Grab it,
Steal it,
Take it away!
We want the ball
To go the other way!

Eagle Spirit

In the air
On the ground
Eagle spirit
Is all around!

On the Boards

Eagles get on the boards
Put it through
For two!
Score, Eagles
Score!

Go, Team, Go

Ready, hey!
Go, team, go
Go, team, go
Shoot 'em high,
Shoot 'em low,
Yeah team . . . let's go!

Get That Ball

Get that ball
Raise the score
Get that ball
We want more
Get it . . .
Sink it . . .
RAISE THAT SCORE!

Extra

Extra, extra
That's our team
Extra fast with
Lots of steam
Extra special team
EAGLES!

Victory

Victory!
Victory . . .
Is only a step away
We've moved to the top . . .
And we can't be stopped
'cuz victory's on its way!
Said VICTORY!

Up in the Air

Up in the air
And over the rim
Come on, Bob
Put it in!

On a Spree

Look at the Eagles
They're on a spree
Headin' down the court
For a victory!

Trying Hard

We're trying hard
To be the best
We'll never give in till
We meet our quest
Trying hard!

We've Got a Goal

We've got a goal
That goal is to win . . .
In order to reach it
Get a basket again!

Tip Top

Now here's a tip
Our team's on top
We always win . . .
We never stop!

The Biggest Team

We're the biggest team
You've seen
We're the biggest
And we're awfully mean
Eagles are
The biggest team!

Down the Court

Let's go, Eagles
Down the court!
Move that ball, Eagles
Down the court
Down, down, down the
    court!

Call Your Bluff

The Eagle team will call
    your bluff
They're always willing to
    show their stuff
Watch us . . . call your bluff!

Are You Ready?

Are you ready? Yeah!
Are you ready? Yeah!
We can't be beat
Won't take defeat
Are you ready? Yeah!

Tonight Is the Night

Tonight is the night
The time is now . . .
The Eagle team will show
    you how
Tonight is the night!

Rebound

Rebound Blue,
Rebound White,
We want a victory,
Tonight!

Big Fight

Let's have one big fight . . .
(crowd yells): FIGHT!
We're gonna win
Tonight!

First Rate

The Eagles are good
The Eagles are great
The Eagles will always be
FIRST RATE!

Fight Hard

The Eagles fight hard
They are always working
Never smirking
The Eagles . . .
Fight hard!

Put It Together

Put it together
For a victory tonight . . .
Show those Trojans
How the Eagle team fights!
Put it together!

Drop It In

Pass that ball
Drop it in . . .
Central Eagles,
Win, win, win!

Gotta Team

The Eagle team fights . . .
They play just right!
And you'll believe us . . .
When we win tonight!

Red Hot

The Eagles are red hot
The Eagles don't miss a
    shot!
Red hot Eagles!

Do It To It

Do it to it
Take that ball
Towards that goal
Show the Trojans
You've got soul
Do it to it!

Movin' Down the Court

We're movin' down the court
Just as fast as can be
The mighty Eagle team
Lookin' for a victory!
We're movin'!

Aiming for the Top

The Eagles
Are aiming for the top
We don't plan to ever stop
Eagles . . .
Aiming for the top!

Back the Attack

Back the attack
Don't take no slack
The Eagles
Are back!

Eagles Will Fight

Eagles fight!
Use your might!
We will win. . . .
And triumph again!

Get That Ball

Get that ball
Raise that score
Get that ball
We want more!

Stomp Your Feet

Stomp your feet . . .
Keep the beat
The Eagle team
You're about to meet!!
Gooooooooo Eagles!

Wrestling Cheers

Check Him

Check him
Fight him
Never give up
Never give in
Check him!

Sure to Win

John, John sure to win!
Take him down . . .
And get that pin!

Takedown, Reversal

Takedown, reversal . . .
Or go for the pin!
Stay off the bottom . . .
In order to win!
You gotta ride 'em, roll
   'em . . .

Get that pin!
Come on, Mike! Let's win!

Want to Win

Do it, Scott
We want to win
Take your man . . .
Let's pin!

We're the Eagles

We're the Eagles
And you know
That our matmen
Will give you a show!
We are the Eagles!

Take Him Down

Take him down . . .
Turn him over . . .
Go, Eagles, go!

Takedown

Takedown,
Reversal
Show your stuff
Powerful Eagle men
Are really tuff . . .
TAKEDOWN!

Meet the Test

Eagle matmen
Can meet the test
Eagle matmen
Are the best!

Pin 'em

Pin, pin, pin 'em to the floor
Up, up, up the score
Whose score? Our score!
Go! More!

You Can Do It

You can do it!
We know you can!
We're gonna watch you

Take your man!
You can do it!

Really Fight

Go Eagles, go . . . really
   fight!
Go Eagles, go . . . win
   tonight!

Go, Fight, Win

Go (X), fight (X), win (X)
We want a pin!

Hold Him

Hold him . . . hold him
Never give in!
Hold him . . . hold him
Fight to win!

Take Your Stand

Take your stand
What you are is an Eagle
   man!
Come on, Scott,
Take your stand!

Let's Pin

Let's pin (clap, clap)
To win (clap, clap)
Let's pin to win!
Let's do it again!

Strive to Win

Strive to win
And win them all!
Come on, Mike
Get that fall!

Pin Your Man

Pin, pin, pin your man!
You know, you know,
You know you can!
So pin your man
You know you can!

Take Your Stand

Hey, Bob
Take your stand!
Show us you're an Eagle
    man!
PIN!

Roll Him Over

Roll him over
Pin him flat
Show that Viking
Where it's at!
PIN!

Turn 'em Over

Turn 'em over
Show 'em the lights
Come on, Tom
Fight, fight, fight!

What's Happenin'?

Hey, what's happenin'? *X No*
Whatcha gonna do?
Take down, Scott!
We want two!

Takedown

We want a takedown!
Takedown! Takedown! *X*
We want a takedown,
We want two! (XX)

Get That Fall

Mike Collins, hear our call!
Mike Collins, get that fall!
We want to win, come on,
    Mike,
PIN!

Get That Fall

Hey, Bob
Get that fall
Show that Viking
You've got it all!
Get that fall!

Flat to The Mat

Hey, Bob
Pin him
Flat to the mat
Show the Vikings
Where it's at
Flat to the mat!

Now Is the Hour

Now is the hour
To show your power
Roll him over again
Go, fight . . .
PIN!

Hey, Wrestler

Hey, Bob
Fight, Bob
Victory tonight . . .
Right!

Fight

Hey, Eagles
Go tonight
(clap, clap) Fight!
Mighty fightin' Eagles
All right!

Proud to Be

We, the Eagles
Are proud to be
Getting it together
For a victory!

Put Down

We won't be put down
We can't be put down
The Eagles, the Eagles
Are victory bound!

Win Tonight

Win tonight
We want a win *X*
Tonight
Go Do,
Fight,
Win, TONIGHT!

Muscle and Might

We possess
Muscle and might
Our aim is success *X*
So hustle,
And fight!

Watch Out

Watch out!
Our team is rough
And tough
Watch out!

Raise That Score

Raise that score
Mighty Eagles want more
S C O R E!
SCORE!!!!!

Right On

Right on, Blue and Gold
We want to win tonight
Make it happen, Eagles
Victory . . . RIGHT!

Once and for All

Take him down
Once and for all
Take him down . . .
Get that fall!

Gotta Win Tonight

Take him down (XX)
Hold him tight *X*
Take him down (XX)
Gotta win tonight!

We're on Our Way

We're on our way
To victory
We're the best
As you can see
We're on our way

Go, Eagles

Go, Eagles . . .
Get a pin!
Go, Eagles . . .
Go, fight, win!

Make 'em Fall

Hit 'em hard (XX)
Make 'em fall (XX)

Twist

Wrestle . . . wrestle (XX)
Twist him like a pretzel!

Uptight

Uptight (XX) Outasight (XX)
Pin tonight!

Takedown

T-A-K-E-D-O-W-N
Takedown (X)
Takedown!

Take the Mat

Take the mat
Show them who's best
Put them to the test!

Win This Meet

Who's gonna win this meet?
EAGLES
Who are we gonna beat?
Trojans!

Reversal

Reversal
Make him relinquish the mat
We know you can do it
So pin him flat!

Big Pin

Big pin
Let's go, John
Win!
We know you can do it
So PIN!

In the Air

In the air
Or on the mat
The Eagle men
Will knock you flat!

Take the Mat

Take the mat, big Eagles
Show them who is best
Take the mat, big Eagles
And put them to the test
Eagles . . .
Are the best!

Where It's At

Pin 'em to the mat (XX XXX)
We know where it's at
Pin 'em!

Strive to Pin

Strive to pin
Hey-y-y . . .
'A work it out!

Mighty Matmen

The mighty matmen
Will show their strength
They'll show you
Who really rates
Mighty Matmen
Show your strength!

Fight for It

Fight for it
If you want to win
Show your man
That you will pin
Fight for it!

Pin Him Flat

Turn him over (XX)
Pin him flat (XX)

General Use Chants

Hey get up
it's time to cheer
for the ICF spirit is here!

Move it Eagles!
Drive it on down that line
Move it Eagles!
to score is now the time!

Eagles fight
psyche 'em out again!

We've got the rhythm to win
    tonight
TEAM! (X) LET'S (X)
    FIGHT!!

Go Offense!
drive it on through
Eagle team
Score (XX) two!

Relax
We're in control
We'll show you what we can
    do
Relax
We're in control
Eagles coming through!

Knock 'em!
Block 'em!
Push on through
Turkey team
We're after you!

The Eagle team
is super great
we'll take control and
dominate!

PMA Hey!
get it got it go all the way
PMA Hey!
get it got it go all the way!

Use your muscles
stand tall
Use your muscles
don't fall!

Get into the groove
ICF is on the move

A.M. A.M.
is absolutely motivating
Good morning everybody
(X) let's cheer!

We're fired up
We're sizzling
we can't be stopped
come on mighty Eagles
take it to the top!

score!
score!
score!
score Eagles score!

G—o Go (XX)
let's go!

Roll your body
and move your feet
stand up everybody
and get that ICF beat!

Hey where's the beat
that ICF beat
that ICF beat
that keeps you on your feet!

What time is it?
It's time!
What time is it?
It's time!
to go!
to fight!
it's time to win this game
   tonight!

I I love to cheer
C See you next year
F For ever cheer
ICF!

Lets go
Lets go
let your spirit show!

M-O-V-E
Move it for a touchdown
TD!

B-A-S-K-E-T
Basket for a victory
so shoot! shoot! shoot!

Fight for a victory
Eagles going to win
and can't be beat!

V-I-C-tory!
V-I-C-tory!

Up-with-the Eagle pride
I said, up-with-the Eagle
   pride!
Heh-heh-heh!

Lift your head and hold it
high!
A mighty Eagle is passing
by!
Heh-heh! (XX–X,X)
Heh-heh! (XX–X,X)

We got *Power*, we got *Might*
Eagle team is outasite!
Hey-heh (XX) Heh-heh (XX)

P (X) R (X) I-D-E!
We got pride (XX) on our
side! (XX)

Ahhh ya dit it! Now you're
gonna get it!

Mighty, mighty, mighty-
mighty Eagles
go-oooh ah (X) Oooh-ah!

Eagles are the best, Uh-
huh!
Eagles (XX) Have it (XX)
Spirit (XX) Hear it! (XX)

We've got pride! (XXX)
Deep inside! (XXX)

V-I-C-T-O-R-Y!
Eagle team will do or die!

We are the Eagles and the
Eagles are great!

Think (XX XX) Spirit! (XX)

Fe-fi-fo-fum! We got spirit;
now you get some!

Uptight—outasight!
go, Eagles—fight, fight!

Eagle pride known far and
wide!

We've-got-spirit!
Heh-louder, heh-louder!

We're Eagles and-we're-
proud (pause)
Shout it loud—Proud!

Go! Go! Go-go go go-go!
Eagles—!

Rock 'em Eagles, Sock 'em
Eagles!
Go-Eagles-Go!

You gotta work hard, work
hard,
work hard . . . WORK!

1-2-3-4
What the heck we fightin'
for?
POWER . . . power . . .
power!!!

Say, what? Do it to 'em!

The Eagles are fine, so fine
(XX)

ASK: How do you feel?
ANSWER: I feeeelll good!
do do, do do, do do, do . . .
ugh!

Never give up, never give
in!
Fight to win!

Who ah, who ah, who ah
we?

We ah, we ah, we ah the!
E-A-G-L-E-S! Eag-gles! The best!

Hey, *Hey,* Sock it to me now . . .
One more time!

So tighten-it-up—Sock it to 'em now
. . . one more time!

Go! Roust 'em, Fight!
Go-beat-'em NOW!

Our Eagles are red hot . . .
(Stomp-stomp-X)

We got soul
We're super bad!

Number one spirit (X)
Hey let's go! (X)!

Hey! (X) Let's *hear* it! (X)
We've *got* that *Eagle* spirit! (X)

We've got spirit, yes we do!
We've got spirit, how 'bout you?

We've (X) Got (X) Spirit
(XX XX)

Do it! Prove it! We've got might!
Do it! Prove it! Win (X) tonight!

Don't give up! Don't get uptight!
Vict'ry is ours tonight!

V-I-C-T-O-R-Y
Victory, Victory is our cry!
You can do it if you try . . .
V-I-C-T-O-R-Y!

Trojans can't win! We'll do 'em in!

(X) Hey (X) Hey-y (X)
We wa-a-n-n-t (X) a victory!

Strive (X) to (X) win—
Hey-y-y-'a-work-it-out!

Hey, South—South Hey!
Eagles—gonna win today!

Ah-ah-ah-ah-GO! (XX XX)
Ah-ah-ah-ah-GO! (XX XX)

Big-G! Little-O! Go! Go!

Here we go, Eagles! Here we go! (XX)

You're lookin' good, big team!
You're lookin' good! (XX)

Go-Go! Gettum-Gettum! Go! Go!

Get-with-it-now! Go! Go-Go!

Say it loud! We're Eagle proud!

Rip 'em up! Team 'em up!
Go Eagles, Go!

Let's go, let's go!
L-E-T-S-G-O!

One play! All the way! (X)
Let's go!
Get rough! (X) Be rough! (X)
Go! (X)

The word is out so let's shout!
Go, go, go, GO!

Knock 'em down! Tear 'em up!
Go Eagles, go!

Go-Go!
Beat-Beat!
Victory-Victory! Not defeat!

Rah! Rah! Hey! Hey!
Eagle victory all the way!

Fire up! (XX) For victory!

We don't mess around—
we're victory bound!

V-I-C-T-O-R-Y!
That's the Eagle battle cry!

In the air! On the ground!
Spirit—is all around!

Go, Eagles! use your might!
We-want-a-victory (pause) tonight!

NNNNNNobody messes with the Eagle team!

Let's go Eagles! Eagles let's go! (XX)

Y-E-L-L! Come on everybody yell!

The Eagles are here . . .
beware (X)

Go gogo gooo—you mi-ighty Eagles!

F-I-G-H-T! Fight-team-fight! Heh!

Tighten up, team, tighten up!

This (X) is (X) Eagle territory!

I-want-you-to show that you've got spirit!

Rally, rally—oomp-ahh!

S-C-O-R-E Scor-ore! Scor-ore!

Get (X) that (X) ball! (X,XX)

We gotta win! We gotta win!
(X) Let's win!
(XX XXX XX-XX) Let's go!
S-C-ORE! MO-RE (Faster
each time) (XX)
Heh-heh-heh—HUSTLE!!!
HUSTLE !
(All stand) RAH!!!
All my life I wanna be an
Eagle!
Work, work! Oh baby, work!
Work!
All my life I wanna be an
Eagle!
Oomp-ahh! We gotcha!
Ooomp-ahh! We gotcha!

Cheerleaders: Spirit, spirit
. . . we need more!
Pep Club: Team, team . . .
raise that score!

Fire up (XX) With spirit! (XX)

Ooh-ahh! Son of a gun!
The Eagle team is number
one!

1-2, 3-4-5, show your spirit
. . . come alive
6-7, 8-9-10, come on now,
do-it again!

For Central Trojans it's plain
to see!
We're on the road to victory!

Raise that score, raise that
score!
Come on-Eagles, we want
more!

We want (stomp-X) more!
Score!

Let's go defense, let's go!
(XX)
Spirit, spirit! We want spirit!
S-P-I (XXX) R-I-T! (XXX)

Heh-heh! Heh-heh-Eagles!
You look—so good to me!

A great big "V" for victory!

Ahh—Well you can bet (X)
Ya ain't seen nothin' yet!

Say-hey, We got the beat!
Say-whoop! We got the
beat!

Celebrate! Celebrate!
Eagles . . . are really
great!!!

We got the fever, We're hot
We can't be stopped!
(Half of your group is
chanting simultaneously:
We got the
feeeeevvvveerrr!)

Stand up (XX), give a cheer
(XX)
The Eagles (XX) are here
(XX)
Stand up, give a cheer
The Eagles are here!

We've got it (X), now keep it
(X)
Don't lose it (X), we need it!
(X)
Spirit! (X XX) Spirit! (X XX)

Action, action! We want
action!
A-C-T! (XXX) I-O-N! (XXX)

You may be rough, heh
You may be tough, heh
But mighty Eagles, heh
Don't take that stuff, heh
You may be right, heh
You may be wrong, heh
We'll beat you bad, heh
And send you home, heh!

Are you ready! (Ready!)
Are you ready? (Ready!)
Ready (X) for victory!
Ready (X) for victory!

Lift your head up to the
sky . . .
The mighty Eagles are
passing by,
And if you heard what I just
said,
Down on your knees and
bow your head!

S-P (XX) I-R (XX) I-T (XX)
Got spirit? (XX) Let's hear it!
(XX)

1-2-3-4-5 . . . Eagles don't
take no jive!
oohh-ahh we got the spirit!
6-7-8-9-10 . . . Eagles will
do it again!
oohh-ahh let's really hear it!

2-4-5-8-10 . . . come on,
team
let's do it again!
For (X XX) the Eagles! Yeh!

Hey, you—out in the
crowd . . .
If you feel it in your
fingers . . .
Then clap out loud!
Well, can you dig it? (rapid
claps)

We, the Eagles, walk in style
And if your heart can take it
Come soul awhile—!

Eagles in the groove . . . ah
let's move!
We, the Eagles of Central
High
We're gonna win this game
tonight
(pause) And that's no lie!
I said all right, pow,
you can't stop us now!
I said all right, pow,
you can't stop us now!

When you're workin' with the
Eagles
It's mmmmmm . . . so
nice—to work—
alright!

Show me the Eagles!
Show me the Knights!
It's easy to see that we'll win
tonight!

Eagles (X) are (X)
supermen! (X)
And (X) they're (X) going to
win (X)
They're going to win!

Get ready to go! Get ready
to fight!
Get ready you Trojans—
We're winning tonight!

We're from Central and
couldn't be prouder!
and if you can't hear us,
We'll yell a little louder!

Up (X) with (X) Eagle pride!
I said, Up with Eagle pride!
Hey-hey-hey!

Hey! (X) Hey-hey (X) Better
Beware!
Eagle spirit is everywhere!

Shout—out it at the top!
Le—et 'em know we'll never
stop!

Power knocks 'um under!
Power like a thunder!
Eagles have that power!
We're the might Eagles . . .
uh-huh!

Everybody listen—
Get your legs a kickin'
Come on everybody—
Do the funky chicken!

Hehhehheh GOLD! Heh
Blue!
You sure know what to do!

Ain't nuthin' to it
The way we do it
It's so easy to learn
Just stomp your feet
Get in the beat—
Go ahead and burn!

To the left (XX)
To the right (XX)
Left-right-left (XX)
My back is aching
My belt's too tight
My hips keep shaking
From left to right . . . (start
over)

Ahhh—(X)
Let's go, Heh
Alright! Heh
You need (echo) To be
(echo)
A MIGHTY (pause) EAGLE!

WE! (echo)
WE DON'T (echo)
WE DON'T MESS! (echo)
WE DON'T MESS
AROUND—HEY!
WE DON'T MESS
AROUND!!

Have you got that rhythm?
(Stomp-stomp XX)
Have you got that beat?
(Stomp-stomp XX)
Have you got that rhythm?
(Stomp-stomp XX)
Then stamp yo' feet!
(Stomp-stomp XX)
Well, we know some
Eagles!
(Stomp-stomp XX)
And we think they're neat!
(Stomp-stomp XX)
If they keep that rhythm!
(Stomp-stomp XX)
They'll never be beat
(Stomp-stomp XX)
B(X)E(X)A(X)T(X)
We got the beat! (pause)
(Stomp-stomp XX)
B(X)E(X)A(X)T(X)
We got the beat! (pause)
(Stomp-stomp XX)

We're gonna go hi-igher!
(hi-igher!)
We're gonna go hi-igher!
(hi-igher!)
We're gonna go higher-
higher-higher-higher-higher-
WHOO!

Keep the faith Go!
Oh mi-ighty Ea-agles!
Alright, alright—!
Alright-alright-alright—heh!

Charge up . . . get goin'
again
Never give up . . .
Never give in!

Say what's your name?
EAGLES!! (repeat above 3
times)
Gonna live and die for
Central High

Is everybody here? Heh-
heh-heh!
Let me hear you cheer!
Heh-heh-heh!
Eagles in the front, Heh-
heh-heh!
Let me hear you grunt! Heh-
heh-heh!
Eagles in the middle, Heh-
heh-heh!
Let me see you wiggle!
Heh-heh-heh!
Eagles in the rear, Heh-heh-
heh!
Let me hear you cheer!
Ahhhhh . . .
I feel a breeze, heh
It's in my knees, heh
It's in my back, heh
That's where it's at, heh
It's in the air, heh—it's
everywhere, heh!
IT'S ALL OVER, HEH—
IT'S ALL OVER!

Eagles in the groove (XX)
ah let's move!
Uh-we got the power!
Uh-we got the power!

Uh-we got the power!
Uh-and when we *walk* . . .
We got the power to walk
that walk!
And when we *fight* . . .
We got the power to do it up
right!
And when we *talk* . . .
We got the power to talk
that talk!
And when we *scream* . . .
We got the power to make
your heart sing!
We got the power!
Uh-we got the power!
Uh-we got the power!
Uh-we got the power! . . .
UH!

You gotta go, by golly, gotta
go—
You gotta go, by golly, gotta
go—heh, heh!
—FIGHT!
—WIN!
So let's go-fight-win—HEY,
HEY!!

Whoopee, whoopee
Bang, bang
Ea-gles are doin' their thing
Coming on strong . . .
Right on—right on!!!

Um-umgawa, Eagles got
the power
Say, um-umgawa, Eagles
got the power
Say, bang-bang
  Choo-choo train
  Come on Eagles, do your
thing!

We're the roughest team
you've met (XX)
We're the toughest team
you bet (XX)
We're the EAGLES
So you better get set—
'Cause what you see is
what you get!!

Right on, Eagles
Marching on to victory
Right on Eagles
Out to get the enemy
Right on, Eagles, full of
energy!
Right on (X)2(X)3(X)4(X)
Right on (X)2(X)3(X)4(X)!

Eagles are dynamite—
Uptight-and-outasite!
Sock it to 'em, Eagles! Ooh-
ah!

Strive-to-win
Heh—a work it out!
A work . . . a work it on out!

Heaven help the other team
Eagle men are tough and
mean
Go gettum-uh uh-go gettum

Are you ready
To move right down?
Are you ready
Don't just sit around!
Let's all get movin' to
Raise that score
So get ready for a whole lot
more!

We're the mighty Eagles
From Central High
We'll show you how it's done
And that's no lie!

Go-uh uh uh
Fight-uh uh uh
Win-uh uh uh
Do it again!

We're so great
We're so fine
We'll beat the Trojans
Just any old time!

R-I-G-H-T O-N
Come on, Eagles,
Let's win!
Right on, right on!

Winning is a pleasure
That few can enjoy!
So when the Eagles
Get their mind set . . .
Forget it!
Forget it!

Boogie to the left
Boogie to the right
We're gonna conquer
The Trojans . . .
Then boogie all night!

We're gonna fight, fight,
fight
All the day
We're gonna win . . .
That's what I say!

Hey, watch your step now
We're on our way
We'll fight you right
Anytime night or day!
Watchout, Watchout,
Watchout!

The Eagles, the Eagles
  the Eagles are on the
move!
The Eagles, the Eagles,
  the Eagles are in the
groove!

The Eagles (XX) have power
(XX)
The Eagles have plenty of
power!

The Eagles are tough! (XX)
The Eagles are su-per
tough!

The Eagles are great! (XX)
The Eagles are really great!
(XX)

Eagles keep fightin'
  when the goin' gets tough
  (repeat three times)
Eagle team (XX) tough
enough!!

Two for the price of one,
plus a dollar!
All for th Eagles, stand up
and holler!

Heh-heh! (XX, XX)
Heh-heh! (XX, XX)

Let's do it, Eagles
Let's do it right
You got the spirit
You got the might!
Let's do it—do it right!
(XXX)

There's no time like the
present
And the present's right now!
So explode on the whistle
With a zap, bang, pow!

Well alright, well alright, well
alright! Heh-heh!

We can't do no wrong
'Cause we're the mighty
Eagles
And we're rollin' along!

We wanna go, we wanna go
tonight
We wanna fight, we wanna
fight tonight
We wanna win, we wanna
win tonight
We wanna go
We wanna fight
We wanna win . . .
TONIGHT!
Eagles . . . alright!

Central Eagles! Central
Eagles!
Swingin' along lookin' cool
and calm!
And sayin'
 ooh-ahh! We got you!
 ooh-ahh! We got you!
 ooh-ahh! We got you!

The Trojans have somethin'
that no other team has!

(repeat three times)
And that's nothin',
absolutely nothin!
Positively nothin' (XX) That's
what!

Go get 'em! Uh huh!
Go get 'em! Uh huh!
Go gettum-go gettum-go
gettum!
 Uh! Uh! Uh!

I said heh, heh you!
There's nothin' you can do—
You just can't stop the
Eagle machine!

Who are the Eagles?
 We are the Eagles!
What kind of Eagles?
 Fighting Eagles!
What kind of Eagles!
 Fighting Eagles!
What kind of Eagles?
 Winning Eagles!

Clap your hands (clap)
Clap your hands (clap)
Get it together (clap, clap)
Everything's alright

Clap your hands (clap)
Clap your hands (clap)
Get it together (clap, clap)
We're gonna win tonight

Get it on Big Blue (clap)
Get it on big White (clap)
Get it on in the morning
(clap, clap)
Get it on at night

Lay that spirit on me
Lay that spirit on me
To be a great team, you
gotta
Have some!
So lay that spirit on me!

What's the word in the
passing hour?
Keep on trucking with Eagle

power
Shove that ball across the
line
Eagle team . . . gonna blow
your mind!

Eagles gonna rock (whoo!)
Eagles gonna roll (whoo!)
Eagles gonna rock,
Eagles gonna roll,
Eagles gonna rock and roll!

We know . . . that *we are* . . . the *best!*

We want . . . *we* want MORE!

Trojans are the team that we're
 gonna defeat!
So come on, everybody, get the
 Eagle beat!

Trojans are the team that we're
 gonna defeat!
So come on, everybody, get the
 Eagle beat!
Take time (XX) and just relax! (XX)
We're number one (XX)
And that's a fact! (XX)

Eagles in the lead! (X)
Eagles (X) got all the speed!

Shape 'em up, Eagles
Ship 'em out! (XX)

Eagles are the best! (X)
Best of all the rest! (X)

Stop, look, and listen—
Here come the mighty Eagles!

Come on Eagles! (X)
Let's have some action!

Well . . . the team is on the flo-or
(stomp-clap, stomp-clap-clap)
And the Floor is ho-ot
(stomp, claps)
Ah, well we can't lo-ose
(stomp, claps)
We got the fever, we're hot
We can't be stopped!

The Eagles are here, beware! (X)

All you gotta do is put your mind to it! (X)
Buckle down, buckle down!
Do it, do it, do it!

Eagles tough, we got stuff!

Get on up (XXX)
And work it out! (XXX)

No, No! Never, never! Uh-uh-uh!

When the season's done,
We'll be Number One!

We hate defeat! (XXX)
We won't be beat! (XXX)

Charge up! (XX) get goin again! (X)
Never give up (X) Never give in!

We're number one, we're-gonna-keep-it-
   that-way! (XXXX)

Jam up and jelly tight!

Come on, mighty Eagles,
Get down and fight!

Clap your hands! (clap, clap, clap)
Stomp your feet! (stomp, stomp, stomp)
Central Eagles can't be beat!

Get tough! (XX) Hurry up! (XX)

Can't be beat! (X) Can't be beat! (X)
All for Eagles, 'a repeat!

Fight-fight! Fight-fight-fight!
We're gonna win-this-game tonight!

Heh . . . BLUE
Heh . . . GOLD
Heh . . . TEAM (XX) Let's go!

Who's gonna win tonight?
Eagles are gonna win tonight!
Heh (X) Heh (XX)
Heh (X) Heh (XX)

Eaaa-gles!
. . . GO!
   . . . FIGHT!
   . . . WIN!
GO-FIGHT-WIN!

AHHHHH--------Boom!
Eagle cry! Eagle cry!
Heh-heh! Eagles!

Well, it's all-lll-right!
Ea-gles keep it toge-ther!
Mighty, mighty, mighty, mighty, mighty mighty mighty mighty,
Mighty-mighty Eagles! Whew!

Hey, gang! What?
Hey, gang! What?
Spirit! What?
SPIRIT—S-S SPI! (XX XXX)
   R-R RIT (XX XXX)
SPI (XXX) RIT (XXX)
Spirit! Spirit! Yeahh—spirit!

(fast)
   Who's gonna win-win?
   Who's gonna win-win?
   Who's gonna win-win, now?
   We're gonna win-win!
   We're gonna win-win!
   We're gonna win-win, how?
(slower)
   E-A-S-Y EASY!
   Hey, South thinks they're cool
We know Central is the number one school!

Is everyone happy?
H-A-P-P-Y! Yeah!

When all the rest have given up
The Eagle team's on top! (XX)

Let's break the tie (X)
Central High (X)

It matters to us! It matters to you!
Central Eagles, pull us through!

Victory-victory, say it loud (XXX)
Central won and (pause) we're proud!

We're gonna rock 'em up and
Rough 'em up and win to-night!

Are you ready for a Central victory,
'Cause we are ready for you! (X X X)

Let's get that ball (XX)
Let's get that ball! Fight-fight!

Make that score go higher, higher!

Come on Central, do your best!
Keep on fighting for C.H.S.!

Now's the hour! Use your power!
Go team, go!

Fire up, Eagles!
Fire up-and-score!

With plenty of might and lots of fight!
Get with it! (XX) Get with it! (XX)

Fight hard (X) don't stop (X)
We're rising to the top! (X)

That's okay! That's alright!
Stay in there and fight!

We know you-can-do-it!
We know you-got-might!
So come on team let's fight! (X)

Hey! (X) Big-team! (XX)
Pull through! (X pause X)

Hey-hey we fight! (XX) To win! (XX)
We never give in!

Fight 'em big Blue, fight 'em! (XX)

We're the greatest! We're the best!
We're the team from C.H.S.!

That's good (X) that's good (X)
Now we're playing like we should!

Ready, set? (XX) You bet (XX)
What for? (XX) To score! (XX)

We're (X) proud (X) of-ourrr-team! (X)
We're-proud-of-our-team!

Teamwork! Teamwork! (XX XXX)

Hey, you! Over there!
   Stand up and start-to-cheer!
Get-get get-get get-get get on up!
Whoo! Hey gogo gogo gogo
Get on up! Whoo!

Lean to the left! Lean to the right!
Stand up, sit down! Fight-fight-fight!

Hey-hey! Look at that score!
That's okay, but we want more!

Get that ball and raise that score!

Yell! (yell!) Scream! (scream)
Let 'em know! (let 'em know!)
We're for that team! (we're for that team!)

Hey-go! (XX) Hey-fight (XX)
Go (X) Fight (X) Win (X) Tonight!

Keep-it-up, big team, keep-it up! (XX)

Our team is dynamite!
They're gonna win tonight!

The Eagles! (XX) have power! (XX)
The Eagles have plenty of power! (XX)

Turn (X) on (X)
Eagle (X) power! (X)

We've got the power (X) *GO* POWER!

We got the power (X) the might! (X)
So fight, team, fight!

Keep the faith, go! (X)
Oh mighty Eagles!

Be calm . . . (X) be cool . . . (X) . . . be together!

We're gonna rock . . .
   we're gonna roll . . .
   we're gonna beat ya . . .
   with a lot of soul!

We're tough (X), we're rough (X)
We know it and we show it!
We got power (X)
Whoo! Eagle power! Whoo!

We-got the super soul spirit . . . got the S.S.S.!

We're gonna rough 'em up, yeah!
Right on! Right on!
 Eagle machine keeps moving along!
Right on, right on, right on! (XX)

Second to none! We're number one!

Here we come, number one!
We are the best
 and we'll make you run!

We don't care what they say!
We're gonna beat 'em anyway!

Alright! (X)
Alright! (X)
Tonight is our night!

Get up (X), get to it (X)
We know we can do it! (X)

Stand up! (XX) Give a cheer! (XX)
Let 'em know (XX) We're here! (XX)
Stand up, give a cheer,
Let 'em know we're here!

Grrrrreat big Eagles, Eagles are great!

Eagles-on-the-loose!
Aw-aw the-loose!

2-4-6-8 . . .
this-is-the-year-we-go-to-state!

We know, that we are the
 B (X) E (X) S (X) T (X)!

We're number one, Hey!

V-I-C-I-O-U-S! Are we vicious?
Well—yes!

When you're hot, you're hot!
And when you're not, you're not!
And we're hot (XX)
And you're not! (XX)

It's easy to do (XX) It's up to you! (XX)

You are what you are (X)
You can't change that (X)
And where we are is where it's at!

T-O! T-O-U! T-O-U-G-H!—Get tough!

We're the best around, hey!
We're the best around!

Can! Can! We know we can!
Beat those Trojans!

Think (X) Yes (X)
And do-your-best! (X)

I say alright (X) Okay! (X)
That's the Eagle way!

Hey, Eagles (X) you're lookin' good! (X)
Just like (X) I knew you would!

Hey, Bob, take your stand!
Show us you're an Eagle man!

We're-coming-to-get-you-look-out!

Eagles are 'a movin' and we're out to win! (X)

Stand up and show-your-stuff!
Make-'em-see we're really tough!

It's the rockin'est that you can find!
That great Eagle spirit nearly blows your mind!

Do what ya wanna, when ya wanna, how ya wanna!
Say do your thing, get down! Whoo!

Hey, hey! (X)
Get ready, here we come! (X)
Gonna get those Trojans on the run!

Ahhh whatcha say! (X)
Ahhh whatcha say! (X)
Get together now!
Get together right now!

Be (X) aggressive (X)
Be (X) aggressive! (X)
B-E A-G-G-R-E-S-S-I-V-E!

Wo-o-oo-ooooo-oh-oh-oh! WHOO! shoo-bop, sh,
 doobee doobee do!

Said what's your name?
  (Eagles!)
SAID WHAT'S YOUR NAME?
  (Eagles!)
I said they're the pride
  (I said they're the pride)
Of Central High!
  (Of Central High!)

You can sock it to the East!
You can sock it to the West!
But when you sock it to the Eagles
Yeah-man!
You sock it to the best!
1-2-3-4-5-6-7-8
Do that stuff, yeah, do that stuff!

(You gotta win, you gotta win,
You gotta win-win-win!) (three times)
Um-ahhh! Um-ahhhh!

(Gooo-fiiighttt-wiinnnn!) (three times)
Um-ahhh! Um-ahhh! Um-ahhh! UM!

1-2 3-4-5
Eagles are lookin' fine!
Hey-hey, we're lookin' fine, yeah!
2-4 6-8-10
Eagles will win again!
Hey-hey, we'll win again, yeah!
10-8 6-4-2
Eagles we're backin' you!
Hey-hey, we're backin' you, yeah!
5-4 3-2-1
Eagles are number one!
Hey-hey, we're number one, yeah!

Oh you may beat the others,
  and you may beat the rest . . .
But you can't beat the Ea-gles
  'cause we're all set!
You can cool your cool,
  and you can beat your time . . .
But you can't beat the Eagles
  any o' the time!

Just give me a beat! (XX X)
Just give me a beat! (XX X)
Don't need no words,
Don't need no tune,
Just give me a beat!

Well, I walk walkin' down the street
Feelin' mighty fine,
Saw a mighty Eagle
  and I blew my mind!
Hey, hey, mighty Eagles,
You're lookin' good!
Don't need no words,
Don't need no tune,
Just give me a beat!

Now when you're up, you're up,
And when you're down, you're down!
But when you're up against the Eagles
You're upside down!
Hey-hey, mighty Eagles,
You're lookin' good!
Don't need no words,
Don't need no tune,
Just give me a beat!

Two for the price of one plus a dollar!
All for the Eagles, stand up and holler!
Hey-hey (XX XX)
Hey-hey (XX XX)

Two bits, four bits, up to sixteen!
All for the Eagles, stand up and lean!
Whoo-whoo (XX XX)
Whoo-whoo (XX XX)

Two bits, four bits, all around the clock,
All for the Eagles, stand up and rock!
Get down! (XX XX)
Get down! (XX XX)

Say Eagles . . . (say what?)
Say Eagles . . . (say what?)
Let me hear you spell our name!
(What's that you say?)
Let me hear you spell our name!
(What's that you say?)
I say E-A-GLES (XXXX XX)
Ugh huh, Ugh huh

Say Eagles . . . (say what?)
Say Eagles . . . (say what?)
Who's got spirit that's reeally great?
(What that you say?)
Who's got spirit that's really great?

(What's that you say?)
I say E-A-GLES (XXXX XX)
Ugh huh, Ugh huh

Say Eagles . . . (say what?)
Say Eagles . . . (say what?)

Who's gonna win this game
    tonight?
(What's that you say?)
Who's gonna win this game
    tonight?
(What's that you say?)
I Say E-A-GLES (XXXX XX)
Ugh huh, Ugh huh!

We really love those Eagles,
We've got to have those
    Eagles!
We really love them,
Got to have them
Eagle power!

FRESHMEN, FRESHMEN
Don't be shy!
Stand and give your battle
    cry!
V-I-C-T-O-R-Y
THAT'S THE FRESHMEN
    BATTLE CRY!
(repeat with sophomores,
    juniors and seniors)

YOU! (XX) Yeah, YOU! (XX)
Have you (XX) Got Spirit?
    (XX)
Have (XX)
You (XX)
Got (XX)
Spirit? (XX)
(XX XX)—'a we do!

Heh-heh: We've got spirit
    with a capital "S"
Heh-heh: We're really
    pushin' with a capital "P"

Man we're with it!
Heh!
Ho!
(all EAGLE SPIRIT!
A let's go!

Give me an "M" . . . (M)
    "I" . . . (I)
    "G" . . . (G)
    "H" . . . (H)
    "T" . . . (T)
What does that spell?
    Might!
What do we need? Might!
What do we have? Might!
    We got might, yeah
    We're out of sight, yeah
    We may be bold, yeah
    But we've got soul!
Ah . . . let's go!
Ah . . . let's fight!
Ah . . . let's win! (XX)
    THIS GAME TONIGHT!

We're from Central
Haven't you heard?
And when we say beat 'em
A . . . beat 'em's the word!

Go . . .
    'a beat that team—
Fight . . .
    'a beat that team—
Win . . .
    'a beat that team—
GO . . . FIGHT . . . WIN
    'a beat that team . . .
    YEAH!
If you're all for the Eagles,
    stamp yo' feet! (XX)
If you're all for the Eagles,
    if you're all for the Eagles
    . . .
stamp yo' feet! (XX)

If you're all for the Eagles,
    Clap yo' hands! (XX)

If you're all for the Eagles,
    if you're all for the Eagles
    . . .
clap yo' hands! (XX)
If you're all for the Eagles,
    shout hooray! (XX)
If you're all for the Eagles,
    if you're all for the Eagles
    . . .
Shout hooray! (XX)

Central Eagles (XX)
Always win (XX)
They always bring (XX)
A victory in! (XX)
Because of this (XX)
We wanna scream (XX)
    You can't stop (choo-
    choo)
    Our green machine
    (choo-choo)
There's no way
    (bounce, bounce, pop
    mouth)
Heh!

We've got to move . . .
To get into the groove!
We've got to fight . . .
To win this game tonight!

We've got to jump . . .
To get over the hump!
So . . . Go gettum—heh-
    heh!
Go gettum, gettum, gettum,
    hit
    'em—ugh!

Power to the Eagles (XX)
Power to the Eagles (XXX)
Power to the Eagles (XXX)
Power to the Eagles—
    RIGHT ON!

Go (XXX) big Eagles (XXX)
Fight (XXX) uh-huh (XXX)
Go big Eagles!
Fight big Eagles!
Do it—do it!
Alright—alright . . . GO!

The white, the blue,
    are comin' through—
So be mellow, because—
    we're gonna beat you!
B-E-A-T Trojan team,
    so be mellow!

(*crowd repeats these
   lines)
*Everywhere we go . . .
*People want to know . . .
*Who we are . . .
*Where we come from . . .
*Well this is what we tell
   them . . .
   (ending #1):
*We're the mighty Eagles!
   (ending #2):
Who are, who are we?
We are, we are the . . .
The mighty Eagles!

So hard, so hard!
   So hard to be an Ea-gle!

We know the Eagles are
   great (X)
   great! (XXX)

T-O-U-G-H Get Tough (X)
   Eagles!

Trojans on the lose! (X)
Charge! (X) Charge! (X)

Let's get fired up! (XX XXX)

Hey-hey! Hey-hey! (X) Hey
   you! (X)
There's nothin' you can do
   . . .
'Cause you just can't stop
   that Eagle machine!

Ah keep the faith!
Ah keep the faith!
Ah keep the faith!

Right on, right on, right on!
Right on, Eagles!
We've got the spirit,
To get it undone—
Right on, Eagles!
Right on, right on, right
   on!!!

Alright! (stomp X stomp XX
   stomp X stomp XX)

(repeat after each
   "alright")
Alright!
Get it, Eagles—get it!
I—know you can get it!
Get it, Eagles—get it!
   I know you can get it!
Alright!
Alright!
Prove it, Eagles—prove it!
   I—know you can prove it!
Prove it, Eagles—prove it!
   I—know you can prove it!
Alright!
Alright!
Win it, Eagles—win it!
   I—know you can win it!
Win it, Eagles—win it!
   I—know you can win it!
Alright!
Alright!

We got soul (XXX)
We got style (XXX)

We got . . . what it takes!
We're gonna try (XXX)
Our best (XXX)
To win . . . this game
   tonight!
(XXX)

People, people, have you
   heard?
   (YEAH!)
People, people, have you
   heard?
   (YEAH!)
Am I right-or-wrong? (You're
   right!)
Am I right-or-wrong? (You're
   right!)

Bing, bing
Bang, bang
Eagles got the ball!

What do the freshmen think
   about the Eagles?
We think they're alright!
What do the sophomores
   think about the Eagles?

We think they're uptight!
What do the juniors think
   about the Eagles?
We think they're outasite!
What do the seniors think
   about the Eagles?
Oom tay ga . . . oom oom
   tay ga!
Oom tay ga . . . oom oom
   tay ga!
What do you all think about
   the Eagles?
Oom . . . we got it!
Oom . . . we got it!

Freshmen . . . (yeah!)
Are you ready? . . . (yeah!)
Everybody: Well let's go-go!
   Go-go!
   Let's go-go! Go-Go!
Sophomores . . . (yeah!)
Juniors . . . (repeat)
Seniors . . .

Heh-heh-how 'bout it?
   Ahhh-can you shout it?
Heh-heh (X XX) (X XX)
Heh-heh-let's hear it!
We've got Eagle spirit!
Heh-heh (X XX) (X XX)
Heh-heh-how 'bout it?
   Ahhh-can you shout it?
Let's go! E-A-GL-ES—
   EAGLES!

(echo each line)

SAA—TISFIED!
I mean ree—al satisfied!

First you lean to the left!
Then you lean to the right!
And you fight-fight-fight!

Satisfied!
I mean re-al satisfied!

My name is Carol . . . yeah!
And that's no lie . . . yeah!
I'll be an Eagle . . . yeah!
Until I die . . . yeah!

Hooray . . . for Eagles!
Hooray . . . for Eagles!
Someone's on the bus,
Yelling hooray for Eagles!
1-2-3-4 who ya gona yell
    for?
Eagles—that's who—!

We're (XXX) gonna (XXX)
    win (XXX) you know (XXX)
We've got Eagle spirit (X)
We're gonna let you hear it!
    (X)

To the left, to the right,
To the left, to the right, to
    the left (XX)
Our team is movin' . . .
    our crowd's uptight!
Our boys are movin' . . .
    from the left to the right!
Ooh-ahh! We got the spirit,
    heh!
1-2-3-4-5 Ealges keeping it
    alive!
6-7-8-9-10 Eagles will do it
    again!
Ooh-ahh! We got the spirit
    . . . HEH!!!

Heh Eagles, heh baby, heh
Eagles (XXX) (half of crowd)
Ahhh—big Eagles! (other
    half of crowd)

CHORUS:
Get the beat, get the beat,
    get the beat—get the
    beat!
And rock your seats, rock
    your seats, rock your
    seats, rock your seats!

Now, let's get the rhythm
    with the hands (XX)
Now, you get the rhythm
    with the hands (XX)
Now, let's get the rhythm
    with the feet (XX) (stomp)

Fantastic-terrific we got a
    thing
Going on that can't be beat!

Mighty, mighty Eagles—
    may come alive!
Jump in there and jive, jive!

Have you got pride?
Don't hide your pride!
Have you got P-R-I-D-E?
Got pride?
(repeat three times)

Eagles got the spirit, spirit,
    spirit
Eagles got the spirit, spirit,
    spirit
Carry the Eagles' spirit
    wherever you go,
    whatever you do
It's the finest kind of spirit
    . . .
we've got it now . . .
We'll show it to you

Don't escape the fact
That the Eagles are where
It's at!

Football Chants

First and ten! Do it again!
    Go go-go go!

Push 'em back! Push 'em
    back!
Waa-ay back!

Hit 'em again! Hit 'em
    again!
Harder . . . Harder!

Hit that line! Hit that line!
Come on team, you're doin'
    fine!

Eagles-Eagles how 'bout it
    . . .
Lookin' for the goalpost—
    we'll find it!
Yeah, yeah, yeah!
Yeah, yeah, yeah!

'A Eagles! 'A Eagles!
'A doin' fine!
'A take that ball right down
    the line!
'A Eagles! 'A Eagles!
'A what do ya say!
'A touchdown time's right
    away!

Movin' on down, movin' on
    down,
Movin' on down for a
    touchdown!

Block that kick! Heh, block
    that kick!

T-O-U-C-H, D-O-W-N
    Touchdown!

Moving on down the field!
Workin' for six points more!
(XX) Touchdown! (X) Get it!

Down the field, big Blue,
Down the field!

One way, all the way, let's
    go!

Score, score! Six points
    more!

Push 'em back (XX)
Let's attack! (XX)

Hit 'em high! Hit 'em low!
Make 'em fumble! Let's go!

Block 'em, Eagles, hit 'em
    hard!
Make 'em fight for every
    yard!

Hey! Get it and go!

Break! Break!
Break through that line!

Our defense, yeahh—
Is gonna show ya, yeahh—
Just what we got, yeahh—
    So look out! (X XX)

Our defense, yeahh—
Is gonna show ya, yeahh—
Here we come!

Offense-offense! We got
soul!
So keep that ball in control!

Push 'em, push 'em, faster,
faster!
Go-go-go!

1-2-3-4 . . .
Who ya-gonna score for?
E-A-G-L-E-S!
We wanna touchdown!

Hey-Hey! What-do-you-say?
Let's-go-back the-other-
way!

Come on, Eagles, raise that
score!
We want a touchdown (X)
Six more!

Eagles, Eagles, we've got
soul!
Kick that ball right over the
goal!

We want a touchdown, yes
we do!
Come on Eagles,
Let's see what you can do!
Hey!

All-the-way down-the-field
boys!
All-the-way down-the-field
boys!
Let's Go!

Through the line, over the
goal,
Come on Eagles—let's go!

We're with you, Eagles, so
fight!

Yardage (XX) Yardage (XX)

1-2-3-4! What do you think
those cleats are for?

We're the great! We're the
fine!
We're the mighty Eagle line!

Hold that line! Hit 'em hard!
Make 'em fight for every
yard!

Big Red get rough! Big Red
get tough!
Get rough! Get tough! Let's
go!

We wanna, we wanna! (half
of crowd)
We wanna touchdown!
Weeeee—wanna
touchdown!
(other half of crowd)

Six points! (XX)

Touchdown, touchdown! (X)
six points!

End-tackle-center-guard!
Hit 'em, hit 'em, hit 'em
hard!

Heh-hold that line!

Heh-kick that goal!

Basketball Chants

I said shoot (X) the hoop (X)
Shoot, shoot (X) the hoop!

Gotta have, gotta have,
Gotta have two!

We want two! We want Two!

Basket-basket! We wanna
basket!
B-A-S! (XX) K-E-T! (XXX)

We've got the ball—so,
move it!
Move it!
(stomp X, stomp X, stomp
XX)

And the score goes up
another notch (stomp,
stomp XX)
Fight!

S-TE-A-L Steal-it! Steal-it!

T-W-O! Hey two, two!

Come on, let's get it!
Come on let's get a basket!

Get that ball back (X) right
now!

Take that ball right back,
back!
Take that ball right back!

We got the ball, so GO!
GO!

Make (X) it (X) count (XXX)

Steal it, steal it!
Take-it-away! (XX)

Go, Bob! Go! Go!
Make that free throw!

Let's go big Five, let's keep
it alive!

Sink, it, Bob, sink it!
We know you can sink it!
Sink it, Bob, sink it!
We know you can sink it!
Alright!
(stomp X, stomp XX, stomp
X, stomp X, stomp XX)

Jump, jump, jump, high!
Send that ball to the Eagle
side!

Tip it, tip it, tip it to an
  Eagle!

Jump, jump, jump real high!
Get that ball and fight!

Dribble it, pass it! We want
  a basket!

Again, again!
Again-again-again-hey!
  Make it!

That's okay! That's alright!
You can't win unless you
  fight!

That's okay! That's alright!
He's a Trojan full of fight!
Okay! Alright! Fight!

Bob, Bob, hear our call!
Sink it, sink it, sink that ball!

Take your time on the line!
Shoot for two!

That's okay! That's alright!
If you want to win, you've
  got to fight!

1-2-3-4 move that ball
  right down the floor!
Stomp 'em, Eagles, stomp
  'em!

Bob, Bob—hear our plea!
Sink that ball for victory!
S-I-N-K SINK IT!

Steal it, swipe it!
That's the way we like it!

Hey, Bob, grant our wish!
All we want to hear is (XX)
  swish!
Swish it through the basket!
A two points!

Come, let 'er rip! Get the
  tip!

2-4-6-8-10 Come on,
  Eagles, put it in!

Get up (X) on up! (X)
Beat 'em at the jump! (X)
  I said,
Get up (X) on up! (X)
Beat 'em at the jump! (X)

Jump up! (X) Jump high!
  (X)
Don't let that (X) ball get by!
  (X)

Speed up your feet!
Get that ball movin!

Hey! Get it and go!

We want two—we want two!
Eagles! Eagles!
Shoot it through!

There's a lot of action on the
  Eagle floor,
'Cause the mighty Eagles
  are gonna score!

Everyman, check your man,
and don't let him shoot!

Down, down, down the
  floor!
Raise, raise, raise the
  score!
Down the floor, raise the
  score
We want more!

All-the-way down-the-
  court—Go!
Go!
All-the-way down-the-
  court—
  Fight!
Fight!
All-the-way down-the-
  court—Win!
Win!
All-the-way down-the-
  court—
Go! Fight! Win!

Peanuts, popcorn, onion
  soup!
We want a basket through
  the hoop!

You know what to do! Put it
  in for two!

Shoot and score—two
  more!

Put it in the air and over the
  rim!
Come on, Tom, put it in!

Dribble to the basket! Take
  a shot!
Ball goes in and the Eagles
  are hot!
Beat 'em Eagles, beat 'em!

Take your time, on the line!
Steve—put it in!

You can do it!
Sure you can!
You're a mighty Eagle man!

R-I-M! Through-the-rim!
Through-the-rim! Through-
  the-rim!

Hey, Bob! Show 'em how!
Hey, Bob! Sink it now!

Through the hoop, mighty
  Eagles
Through the hoop!

The best team's on the
  floor!
So come on Central (X)
  SCORE!

They've got it, we want it,
Let's take it away!

Heh-heh—wha'dya say?
Someone take that ball
  away!

Heh-heh—where, where?
We wanna basket over
   there!

Beat! Beat! Beat 'em at the
   jump ball!

Dribble it! Pass it! (X)
We wanna basket!

T-A-K-E! Take-it-away! (XX)

Take aw-waay! (XX X XX)
Away from the Trojans! (XX
   X XX)

(Sing-song)
R-e-bo-und! Rebound-
   rebound!
R-e-bo-und! Rebound-
   rebound!
R-e-bo-und! Add it to our
   victory!
Rebound to Central High!

Moovin' ar-round!
Put-it-in-the-basket!
Wee—want! Twwoo—
   points!

Heh-get that ball, go down
   the court
And shoot (pause) shoot!

All-the-way, down-the-court!
   Go-go!
All-the-way, down-the-court!
   Fight, fight!
All-the-way, down-the-court!
   Win-win!
All-the-way, down-the-court!
   Go-fight-win!

I said shoot, shoot!
Shoot through the hoop!

V-I-C-T-O-R-Y Victory
   bound!
Rebound!

T-W-O Say shoot two! Shoot
   two!

Heh-heh! Hey you!
Hey you! Shoot and make
   two!

Shoot 'em high! Pass 'em
   low!
Go-Central-go!

Lightning flash! (XXX)
Spirit roar! (XXX)
The Eagles are on the floor!

And the score goes up
   another point!
(stomp, stomp XX) Whomp
   'em up!

Steal it! Steal it! (XX XXX)

Take it away! (XX) Right
   away! (XX)

See that basket, see that
   rim!
Come on, Eagles—put it in!
Sink-it!

Take-iittt! Away! (XX)
Take it—away! (XX)
Take it-take-it—take it away!
   (XX)

We've got the ball so,
Let's go! Let's go!

Take it away! (XX)

Heh, hey, wha'dya say?
Get the ball! Take it away!

We want a basket! Where?
   There!

S-I-N-K! Sink it, sink it!

Up goes the ball and hits
   the wall
For-a-rebound, rebound (X-
   X)

Two points! (XX)

Basket, basket! (X) Two
   points!

Break that tie! (XX)

Get it up! (XX)
Put it in! (XX)

Put (X) it (X) in! (X-XX)

Heh, Joe, jump a little hi-
   igher!

Beat 'em at the jump!
Beat 'em at the jump!

Up in the air and over the
   rim!
Come on, Bob, put it in!

Jump, you Eagle, jump!

P-U-T-I-T-I-N! Put-it-in! Put-it-
   in!

Hey, we want a basket! Two!
   Two!

All the way, down the floor—
   SCORE!

Movin' on down the floor!
Workin' for two points more!
(XX) Basket! (X) Get it!

Central get that jump ball!
Jump! (X) Jump a little
   higher!

Grab it, steal it, take it away!
We want the ball to go the
   other way!

Shoot in the basket, hey,
Raise that score!
Come on, Eagles, we want
   more!

Hey-hey! Raise that score!
Get that ball, and fight!

Down the floor, raise that
  score
Make it, make it! Two more!

Put (X) it (X) through (XXX)
For (X) two (X) points (XXX)

Set it up (XX) for two points!

Come on team, do your
  best!
Shoot that ball right through
  the net!

V-I-C-T-O-R-Y!
Victory for the big Blue five!

All the way, all the way!
All the way down the floor,
  hey!

Up goes the ball and
  around the rim,
For a basket, basket! (XX)

They've got the ball,
So let's take it away!

Don't give in! We can win!
Come on, Eagles—put it in!

Get up! Get to it!
Get that ball and move it!
Come on, Eagles, score!

Jump-jump! High-high!
Send it to an Eagle guy!

Dowwwwnn! Dowwwwnn!
Gonna get down, gonna get
  down!

Um-gow! Pow-wow!
Give it to us now! Two
  points!

Hey, Bob, you got soul!
So put that ball right
  through the goal!
Sink-that-ball!

G-U-A-R-D Guard your
  man!

Breakthrough for two!
Score, Eagles, score!

We want another one,
Just like the other one!
Basket-basket!

32, 32, make it 34!
  (whatever the score may
  be)

Wrestling Chants

Takedown! Pin 'em—pin
  'em! (X)
Take down! Pin 'em—pin
  'em!

Go, Bob, go! Go, Bob, go!
Pin 'em flat to the mat! Go,
  Bob, go!

V-I-C-I-O-U-S! Are we
  vicious?
Well, yes!

H-U-S-T-L-E! Hustle for a
  victory!

Pin 'em flat to the mat!

John King, hear our call!
John King, get that fall!
We want to win,
Come on, John—PIN!

Hey, Bob, make your move!
Show us you can really
  groove!

Hey, Bob, take your stand
Show us you're an Eagle
  man!

Strive to win and win them
  all!

Takedown, reversal, or go
  for the pin!
Stay off the bottom in order
  to win!
You gotta ride 'em, roll 'em,
  get that pin!
Come on, Bob! Let's win!

Move (X) around, for a—
  takedown!

Roll him over, lay him flat!
Pin his shoulders to the
  mat!

Switch it, change it,
  rearrange it! XX

That's alright, we don't
  mind!
Come on, Bob, you're doing
  fine! (X)
Let's go!

Takedown! Takedown! Two
  points!

Put his shoulders on the
  mat!
We want a pin just like that!

We want to win (pause)
Tom King, pin!
Strive to win, and win them
  all!
Come on, Tom, get that
  fall . . .
Tom, let's win (pause) PIN!

Wrestle, wrestle!
Twist him like a pretzel!

Hey, Eagles, six points for a
  pin!

P-I-N P-I-N Let's pin him,
  hey!

Takedown, get it, get it!

Take him down, take him down,
Take him down and pin—hey!

Hey, Bob, Fight!
Victory tonight—pin!

See that boy, see that mat!
Come on, Bob, pin him flat!

Takedown, Bob, two!

We want five! Don't settle for three!

Don't give in! We can win!
Get in there and P-I-N!

Never give up!
Never give in!
Fight to win! Pin!

Everyman, check your man,
And don't let him pin!

(fast claps) Get! I say get down!

Bob, Bob, hear our plea!
Make this match a victory!

We're behind you, Bob!
Go-fight-pin!

Go-go! Gettum-gettum!
(XX) Pin!

Now's the hour to use your power!
So P-I-N!

We're with you all the way!
Fight-Bob-fight!

Hey-hey-hey!
You're on top and you're there to stay!

Bob's the best—he's on top!
He's gonna pin—he can't be stopped!

Bob is tough, and he's gonna pin!

Pin him now! (XX)
You can do it! (XX)

He's got power! He's got might!
Bob—will pin tonight!

Strive to pin—heyyy 'a work it out!

Uptight! Outasite! Go, Bob!
Pin tonight!

Say what? Do 'em in!
Get in there and P-I-N!

Bob keeps fightin' when the goin' gets tough!
Bob is—tough enough!

Hey, Bob, out on the mat!
Get that man and pin him flat!
Get-get get-get get-get get on up!
Whoo!
Get-get get-get get-get get on up!
Whoo!

Hey, go! (XX) Hey, fight! (XX)
Go! (X) Fight! (X)
Pin tonight!

Get down, get to it!
We know you can do it!
Get down, get to it!
We know you can do it!
Pin! (stomp-clap, stomp-clap-clap,
stomp-clap, stomp-clap, stomp-clap
clap)

Pin your man—you know you can!
Pin your man—you know you can!
Hey, Bob—pin 'em!

V-I-C-T-O-R-Y!
Mike Brown—pin your guy!

Get on up! (XXX)
And break away! (XXX)

Turn him over! Turn him over!
Pin-him-flat!

Turn him over, roll him over
Show him the light—hey!

Two, two, 'a two points!

Let's pin (XX) to win! (XX)

Hustle, Mike! (XX) Let's go!

Pin-pin, pin your man!
You know, you know, you know you can!
So pin your man, you know you can!

Get up! Get goin'!
Really sock it to 'em!

Aw, well you can bet! (X)
You ain't seen nuthin' yet!

Get on up! (XXX)
And stay on top (XXX)
Pin 'em down, pin 'em down,
Put your mind to it!

Reversal! (XX)

Pin 'em! (XX) Pin 'em! (XX)

Break loose! (XX)

We want a takedown! (XX XXX)

Take him down to the ground!

Put him on his back—hey!!

Up and out, Tom, up and out!

Bob, Bob, sure to win!
Take him down and get that
  pin!

I said, come on, come on,
His strength is almost gone!

Hey, what's happenin'?
Whatcha gonna do?
Take down, Tom! We want
  two!

Hey-hey! What d'ya say?
We want a takedown right
  away!

We want a takedown!
  Takedown!
Take-down! We want a
  takedown
We want two! (XX)

Red and White are the
  colors!
Eagles will defeat!
Spirit is the reason—We're
  going to win this meet!

You can do it . . . you can
  win!
Stay in there and pin!

P-I-N, on his back, on his
  back, on his back!
P-I-N, to the mat, to the mat,
  to the mat,
P-I-N, pin him flat, pin him
  flat, pin him flat!
P-I-N to win!

Go-Go! Go-Go! (XXXX)
Fight-fight! Fight-fight!
  (XXXX)

Win
Pin-pin! Pin-pin! (XXXX)
Go! Fight! Pin!

Hey-hey! Get down! Get
  goin'!
Really sock it to 'em!

Pin 'em down, pin 'em
  down,
Put your mind to it!

John, John, sure to win!
Take him down and get that
  pin!

Hold 'em, hold 'em,
Hold 'em to the mat!
F-L-A-T . . . flat! (XXX)

Take him down, take him
  down,
Take him down and pin!
  Hey!

Hey, Bob, do your stuff!
Show us you are really
  tough!

Um umgawa!
Bob's got the power! (XXX)
  To pin!

Move for a takedown!
  Eagles to pin!
T-A-K-E down! (XXX)

Turn him over and show 'em
  the lights!
Hey, Bob, fight-fight-fight!

Bob Murphy, hear our call!
Bob Murphy, get that fall!

Do your warm-ups! Do 'em
  right!
Get on the mat and really
  fight!

We want a pin! Quick!
  Quick!

Do what ya wanna, when ya
  wanna,
How ya wanna!
Say, do your thing!
Takedown—Whoo!

Hey, Bob, Bob Hey!
Hey, Bob, take him down!

S-W-I-T-C-H
Switch right out of there!
  (XX)
We (X) want (X) a pin! (XXX)

Reverse, Bob, reverse!

You-can-do-it, Bob! Yes,
  you can!

Right on-right on!
Takedown-takedown!

Here he comes! He's an
  Eagle!
And he's gonna pin!

Bob's movin' and he's out to
  pin!

The best man on the mat!
Come on, Bob, pin 'em flat!

Takedown, Greg, (X)
  Takedown,
We want a takedown! (X)
Takedown, Greg, takedown!
  (X)
We want a takedown! (X)
You can do it if you try!
Central Eagles never die!
Takedown, Greg, takedown!
  (X)
We want a takedown! (X)

Way down South in
  Dixieland
A mighty-mighty Eagle
  raised his powerful hand
He said . . . we're the best,
  always number one!
We'll be on top when this
  meet is done!
We're gonna go (XX)
We're gonna fight (XX)
We're gonna win this meet
  tonight (X)
Yeah!

Take him down, take him
  down,
Take him down and pin!

Good luck Bob, do 'em in!
We gotta have this P-I-N!

Hey, go! Hey, fight!
Hey, pin tonight!
Hey, go-fight-pin tonight!

P-I-N! Get it! Right now!

Mike is dynamite—He'll win
  this match tonight!

Hey, Red! Hey, Black!
Pin 'em on his back!

Go-go, gettum-gettum!
Go-go, gettum-gettum!
Take 'em down . . . PIN!

Said 'a get down—move
  around!
Pin 'em to the ground!

Mike Collier, don't give in!
Mike Collier—get a pin!

He's tough and he knows it
He's tough and he shows it!
Bob's a tough Eagle man
  and
He always pins his man!

You're in the groove,
You're on the move!
So, go, Bob, go!

Stand up (X) get right (X)
Don't get (X) uptight!
Bob will pin tonight!

Oom pow pow oom pow—
Take him down now!

Tighten up, Bob, tighten up!

Move on the whistle! (XX
  XXX)

Bob's on the move—
Say, Ooh-ahh! (XX)

T-A-K-E! Take 'em down!

Takedown, takedown, take
  two!

Break away! (XX)
Break away! (XX)

20

Where Can You Go from Here?

To some people, cheerleading is like a fever. Once you catch it, the "malady" is hard to shake. It stays with you year after year and can sweep you off your feet at the very first sign of football madness in the early fall. Even people who have been away from the fun of cheerleading for many years have a desire to be "in front" of the crowd rather than up in the bleachers.

For most cheerleaders, several years of cheerleading seems to be enough and the activity ends with graduation from high school. But if it turns out that you want more of cheerleading after high school, there are opportunities that await you. College. Professional sports teams. Instructing future cheerleaders.

Keep in mind that any cheerleading activity past high school will be much more difficult to get involved with, as so many more people will be competing for each position. If you have the right dedication and spirit, however, this disadvantage can be overcome. Here is a description of the three major "post-high school" cheer functions and how you can best prepare for them.

College Cheerleading. While there are more than 34,000 junior and senior high schools in America, there are only about 2,800 colleges and universities that have cheerleading programs. Of these colleges and universities, only 175 are called "major" (that is, large and important on a national scale), according to the National Collegiate Athletic Association. These major schools include such universities as Notre Dame, Alabama, Illinois, Kansas and Texas. At these large universities you have many educational advantages because you can study almost any subject that interests you. At the same time, because these institutions enroll as many as 25,000 to 40,000 students in any year, there will be many people trying out for the cheerleading squad.

Most major university squads are rather large (some having as many as thirty cheerleaders), but in most schools there are as many as fifteen people trying out for each vacant position. And since most big university squads are comprised of both guys and girls, this makes the odds even heavier.

How can you prepare yourself for this? You should begin by looking at the university cheerleading squads in your region. Find out what kind of cheers and routines they use. Do they use gymnastics or partner stunts?

If possible, try to go to some of the games and see the cheerleaders in action . . . and by all means, watch college cheer groups on television when the games are broadcast.

If you decide you definitely want to try out for a major university cheerleading squad, you need to begin in this manner: 1) write to the cheerleading adviser, in care of the athletic director, at the university in which you intend to enroll. Find out from this person the exact requirements for tryouts; 2) become polished in college cheer methods while you are still in high school; 3) be actively involved in various organizations and activities in your high school, and; 4) find out information from every college cheerleader you can find; chances are some graduate of your high school is a college cheerleader right now.

If you can make the squad, the rewards are certainly worth your time and effort. A college cheerleader is an important and recognizable leader on campus. You will be involved in many different campus activities—from homecoming and special alumni events, to giant parades and television appearances. For a lucky few, there are the annual bowl games over Christmas and New Year's holidays, and of course, the many opportunities to travel across the country to away games.

What about cheering for a small college? Across America, there are hundreds of small institutions that enroll as few as several hundred students, and perhaps no more than several thousand. Needless to say, your chances of becoming a cheerleader on one of these campuses are much better than at a large university.

Small colleges generally have good athletic programs and many of them enjoy national reputations. Your crowds are smaller and cheering is really fun. Nearly everyone on campus will know you by name and you will feel you are truly contributing something important to your college. However, oftentimes, cheerleading at a small college is not as advanced in techniques or methods as the major universities. In many ways, cheering at a smaller institution is an extension of what you did in high school.

You should prepare for tryouts at a small college in the same manner as you would for a major university squad.

The choice is yours. Big university or small college. One word of caution: Whatever decision you make should be based on what type of education you are seeking. Cheerleading usually ends completely after college, and unless you have prepared yourself properly in the classroom, even the best cheerleader can miss out on opportunities after graduation. Make cheerleading a warm and memorable "social" activity, but never lose sight of your real priorities in life.

Professional Sports Cheerleaders. In the 1960's, most professional football and basketball teams had cheerleaders, and they actually *were* cheerleaders. They performed in much the same manner as cheerleaders in high school and college.

All of that has changed.

Today's pro sports cheerleader is not, in actuality, a cheerleader at all. She (95 percent of them are female) is part of a chorus line—and is generally selected for beauty, figure, and dance ability. She does not lead cheers, except on rare occasions when the crowd seems to lead themselves in some newly thought-up yell, and she does not wear the standard cheerleading uniform.

Finding out about professional sports cheerleaders is simple. Turn on your television, watch a pro football game and you'll see cheerleaders such as the Dallas Cowboy Cheerleaders. You can find out the requirements for trying out for a particular squad by contacting the team's publicity director. Most generally the qualifications are simple: good grooming, looks and figure, and a reasonably proficient talent in dancing and high kicks.

More than anything else, the pro sports cheerleader is a crowd pleaser, an entertainer. She is there for looks and, quite naturally, her very appearance at a game will help sell tickets. If you decide you would like to try out for such a squad, be prepared to take a radical departure from anything you've ever known about true cheerleading in the past. Big-time sports have very little relationship to athletics on the high school or college level.

The glory and rewards of becoming a pro sports cheerleader are exciting. Television appearances. Immediate recognition throughout the population of a large city. Interviews, ticket-selling drives, banquets and other public appearances. The pay (yes, for once, a cheerleader can actually receive money for doing what she loves to do) is not very much—usually ten to twenty dollars for each game appearance, plus one or two free tickets for family and friends.

Instructing Future Cheerleaders. Once you attend a summer cheerleading camp, you may possibly be eligible at some future date to apply for a position with a company that conducts camps around the country. The job can be one of the most satisfying forms of employment during your school years, for you will have the opportunity to teach young people something you enjoy very much—and you get paid to do it!

The requirements to become a cheerleader instructor include: 1) a demonstrated ability to supervise and work with young people; 2) ability to get along well with others; 3) at least four years of active cheerleading experience; 4) preferably, experience as a college cheerleader, but some instructors are hired directly out of high school; 5) good grades in school; 6) good grooming and appearance; 7) a demonstrated ability to grasp all of the fundamental aspects of school spirit. In other words, you must know everything so you can teach it.

A few individuals are able to continue their cheerleading careers by going to work full time, year 'round, for a cheerleading camp company. But if you are simply interested in a rewarding summer job that will help improve your cheerleading skills while you are helping others, then a position as a cheer instructor is worth seeking.

No matter where cheerleading takes you, or how you pursue it, it is wise for you to keep in mind the true value of what you are doing. Cheerleading is simply not showing off in front of hundreds of your fellow students. It is not achieving popularity that can be lorded over others who weren't fortunate enough to be elected. And it is not just the fun and thrill of leading your athletic teams on to victory.

Cheerleading was developed in the early 1900's and spread quickly across America because it is so much a part of what makes America tick. Cheerleading is part of the "spirit of competition" which has become an important part of our daily lives. It is the desire to be good at something. And it is the will to win in sports.

And just why is cheerleading so important?

Years ago, a young man graduated from a large midwestern university. He had been an average student, participating in a few campus activities and gaining a few good friends. During his years in college, though, he had been an active member of the school pep club, and when he left college as an architectural engineer, he took with him memories that became important to him.

Fifteen years later, this same man (who had only been an average student while in college) had become a millionaire. He ranked at the top of his profession. About this time, his alma mater was asking for contributions to build a new school of architecture and engineering.

This man thought for a few moments about the years he had spent in college . . . they had been the best of his life. He picked up the phone and called the Chancellor of the university. A minute later he had donated *all* of the money needed to build the new building.

Months later, on a rainy day in March and in front of senators, governors and other V.I.P.'s, this man stood and dedicated the building he had helped construct. He said:

"I dedicate this building to the students of this great university, past and present, whose *school spirit* is such that it gives us the will to stay here . . . to study . . . to succeed . . . and to go out in life with both good preparation and fond memories. It is this *school spirit* that is the bedrock foundation of our American educational system."

As a cheerleader, you will play a major role in this great national tradition. Good luck to you!